LIMBO

UNSETTLED QUESTION

George J. Dyer, S.T.D.

FOREWORD BY *Robert W. Gleason, S.J.*

SHEED AND WARD - NEW YORK

Foreword

There are questions in theology which are labelled speculative, metaphysical. Often this implies that, fascinating as they are to the professional theologian, their practical importance, in pastoral work or Christian life, is somewhat limited. The Problem of Limbo is a highly speculative question but also one with high practical import. In an era of ecumenical concern such as ours, where the Christian is fully aware of wide diversity in credal commitments, limbo assumes a distinct importance. When we consider the proportion of the human race who are not baptized, the saving will of God is put in a new light, dependent on our approach to limbo.

So many questions need to be asked about the question of limbo: Is it a doctrine of the Church or simply one more theological opinion? Is it a solution which could be put aside today in favor of more consoling theories? If limbo exists, what precisely is its nature? What relation does the question of limbo have to the salvation of the unbeliever? What was the historical genesis and evolution of this question? Does the perspective in which the question arose and the historical circumstances which surrounded various positions on limbo throw any light on the value of this theological position for present-day thought?

Theologians usually conclude to the existence of limbo from several facts: (1) Baptism, by martyrdom, by water or by desire is necessary for salvation in the present dispensation. (2) But it would seem that an infant is incapable of placing an act of desire, and hence baptism of desire is ruled out, leaving the infant in original sin. (3) The infant who dies in original sin, but without personal sin, will suffer the loss of the Beatific Vision, but not suffer any positive sufferings in addition to that. Fr. Dyer shows how contemporary theologians are divided in their opinions concerning five fundamental propositions related to limbo: (1) its existence; (2) the explanation of the necessity of baptism for infant salvation; (3) the certainty that infants do actually die in original sin; (4) the exact explanation of God's salvific will related to infants; (5) the possibility of baptism of desire for infants.

Father Dyer has undertaken in this book a task of no small difficulty, and has accomplished it admirably. His book seems to me the most comprehensive, judicious *and literate* survey of the problem to date. He has succeeded in untangling the often complicated web of historical circumstances which situated the problem of limbo during the centuries of its popularity. His analysis of documents of the magisterium is exact and penetrating and frequently throws new light on the precise points at issue in these documents.

In addition, *Limbo: Unsettled Question* discusses every notable contribution made by theologians of the last thirty years to the problem of the salvation of infants not baptized by water. This survey is marked by impartiality and sure judgment. The evaluation of theological positions is scholarly, but the scholarship is combined with a delightful felicity of phrase which makes reading a pleasure. To follow the labyrinthine history of the notion of limbo and the theological presupposition it involves with any sort of accuracy is already a major feat. Here this is accomplished with a clarity and ease that will delight both the professional theologian and the ordinary reader who is eager to grasp the main outline of the contemporary debate on limbo and locate the complicated issues at stake with precision. Christians will be consoled to see that an understanding of Limbo is possible which offers a genuine solution to the anguish experienced by those parents who have experienced the trial of having one or more children die without baptism of water. The possibility that infants may be saved by baptism of desire is also explored carefully within the limits of the debate that seem legitimate at the present moment in theology.

Limbo: Unsettled Question is the clearest and most complete treatment of the entire question we know of, and it is pleasant to see how penetration and accuracy are combined with luminous clarity of exposition.

ROBERT W. GLEASON, S.J.

Contents

LIMBO
UNSETTLED QUESTION

Introduction

The death of an unbaptized infant presents us with a poignant problem, and a profound one too. A child is born, draws a breath or two, utters a feeble cry and dies, nameless, unknowing, unknown, like some wandering star that crosses the night sky and burns out before we more than catch a glimpse of it. What does eternity hold in store for such a child? The dawn star of Christian culture had hardly risen when men first asked the question, and their puzzlement has echoed through the centuries. The intense interest of Christian parents has helped to keep the problem alive, but so has the restless curiosity of theologians who failed to find any pat answer in the sources of revelation.

In one sense the problem is a theoretical one; after all, our speculations can hardly affect the child's eternity whatever it may be. But neither is our questioning an exercise in theological pedantry. For the eternity of an unbaptized child is closely tied to several volatile ideas: the existence of original sin, the necessity of the Church, the salvific will of God. Each of these ideas is a vital nerve in the body of Catholic doctrine; and each of them can be studied with almost clinical precision in the person of an unbaptized child. Indeed their fullest implications can hardly be grasped unless we do consider the case of an infant who dies before he can be baptized. If we say that such a child is somehow saved, we have to reappraise the doctrine that the Church is necessary for salvation. If we defend the existence of limbo, we must be prepared to answer those who doubt the sincerity of God's salvific will. A dozen peripheral questions confront us, whatever direction our questioning may take, proving that theology is an organic thing with a remarkable interrelation among all of its members.

Over the centuries there has been a remarkable evolution in theological thinking on the problem of unbaptized infants. Writing in 1954, the English Jesuit Bernard Leeming sketched an attractive solution to the age-old problem. He suggested the possibility of a reunion in eternity of a child and its parents. The parents would enjoy the beatific vision and the child would not, but this would not prevent a free association between them, for heaven is essentially a state of mind, not a place. Fr. Leeming's theory is perhaps best appreciated in the illustration he offers. Let us suppose that a mother and her small son are walking through an art museum. As they walk along hand-in-hand, the youngster is obviously delighted with the shiny marble floors, the brightly lighted rooms, the splashes of color and, most of all, his mother. On the other hand, his mother appreciates all this and much more too. Because of her maturity and her education, she can glimpse in the paintings a whole world of ideas that is closed to the child. Mother and child are in identical surroundings, but with quite a different effect.

We can construct a parallel to this situation in eternity. A child who dies before it can be given the life of grace in baptism never matures as a child of God. In eternity it may possess incomparable human powers of thought and volition, but it has not even begun to mature in the life of grace. On the other hand, the child's mother attained a double maturity at death, not only the fullness of human nature but the full flowering of her intuitive powers as a child of God. In the presence of God she is aware of a boundless world of experience that lies quite beyond the powers of her son. She has matured in the life of grace; he has not. Each is happy but in quite a different way. In Fr. Leeming's view, those who die unbaptized before the use of reason are the children of eternity. And, he asks, who would want a world in which there were no children?

Five centuries ago Dante Alighieri, in his absorbing study of infernal geography, the *Divine Comedy*, gave a somewhat different solution to the same problem. On the fringe of hell, which he saw as a vast crater that pierced the center of the earth, he envisioned a land peopled by those who died unbaptized and before coming to the knowledge of Christ. These men and women of Limbo see clearly what God meant them to be and what they are. But there is no suffering, no despair— only a gentle sadness at the thought of what might have been.

Dante's limbo can be seen in its most primitive form in a catechism written two centuries earlier by Honorius of Autun, from which he derived his imagery. Honorius' *Elucidarium* was used quite extensively throughout Europe during the Middle Ages, serving, apparently, with its simple format of question and answer, as a manual of instruction for the laity. In the "upper hell" in which resided the saints of the Old Testament and the children who died without baptism, the only punishment was "darkness."

However repellent this primitive limbo may seem, it is a thoroughly optimistic departure from a much older view of the problem of unbaptized infants—that of Augustine.

Lashing out against the Pelagians, who denied original sin, Augustine wrote that "those unfortunate children who die without baptism must face the judgment of God. They are vessels of contumely, vessels of wrath, and the wrath of God is upon them. Baptism is the only thing that can deliver these unfortunate infants from the kingdom of death and the power of the devil. If no one frees them from the grasp of the devil, what wonder is it that they must suffer in flames with him? There can be no doubt about the matter: they will go into eternal fire with the devil."

Leeming, Dante, Honorius, and Augustine: these four opinions span fifteen centuries and reveal a whole spectrum of opinion on the subject of infants in eternity. Few ideas have had so remarkable a history, not only engaging at times the greatest minds of Christendom but involving even the Holy See in the clash of opinion.

The past three decades have seen theologians turning to another aspect of the problem—the possible salvation of the unbaptized child. Apparently irreconcilable with the salvific will of God, limbo seems to many to be more the construction of theologians than the working of divine providence. An extensive literature on the subject has appeared in Germany, France, England, Italy, Spain and the United States; not all of it is of equal quality, but seldom has there been evidenced so much dissatisfaction with any of the tenets of theology.

In the chapters that follow, therefore, we will try to trace the evolution of the idea of limbo and the two great reactions to it that have taken place over the centuries—one in the century and a half that followed the Protestant Reformation, the second in our own age.

PART ONE

The Evolution of the Limbo Idea

I

The Patristic Period

AUGUSTINE[1]

Paradoxically, Catholic theology owes a great deal to the heresies of the past. Striking as they did at the heart of the Christian revelation, the heresies forced Christian writers to a reappraisal and a defense of the doctrines under fire. In the fourth and the fifth century of the Christian era men of extraordinary talent were confronted by an extraordinary challenge: and in the fires of the ensuing controversy the golden age of patristic literature was born. Athanasius, Basil the Great, Gregory of Nyssa and Gregory Nazianzen appeared in the Eastern sector of the Christian world to defend the two-fold nature of Christ against the Arians. In the West Augustine wrote unceasingly against the Pelagians, who wanted to declare man's independence of God. The question of unbaptized children occupied a small but persistent part in this debate. Augustine was the first theologian of the West to discuss the problem; and he did so under pressure from the ideas of Pelagius.

PELAGIUS

Pelagius was an unusual man; he almost seems to have been two men: one of them powerful, enthusiastic, almost saintly: the other a timid man, equivocating, toying with the truth in the face of opposition. St. Jerome describes him as a giant stuffed with Scottish pudding, capped by a crag-like forehead.[2] A student from the British Isles, he came to Rome at a moment when history was in labor. Four centuries of duelling with Christianity had exhausted paganism; it was formally proscribed throughout the empire by Theodosius. When the emperors abandoned paganism, a great many of their subjects followed suit. Vast numbers clamored for admission to the Christian Church. Bishops everywhere faced an impossible task in the preparation of these multitudes for reception into the Church: to solve the problem, they decided to baptize first and complete the instruction of their converts afterwards. A great many neophytes regarded their baptism as a talisman, a sort of charm that would ensure their salvation. Once they had been baptized, they felt that they had done all that was necessary for heaven. As a result we find Augustine complaining of the drunkards, thieves, and prostitutes making their way into the Church with no real thought of reform. A pall of indifference to the moral law settled down over a great part of Christianity; the danger of the situation was compounded by a Manichaean fatalism that was seeping in from the East.[3]

Appalled by the lassitude of his fellow Christians, Pelagius tried to infect them with some of the pride he felt in his own human nature.[4] Man, he said, stands at the pinnacle of creation, ruled by his own free will, left to his own free choice. Man is not enslaved by fate or shackled to sin. He is dominated by passion or circumstance only to the extent that he freely submits to them. If he wills to do so, man is quite capable of observing the divine law in all its fullness and of winning the love of God. In his enthusiasm Pelagius envisioned the human race striding through life on a vigorous march toward the distant horizons of human power. That same enthusiasm caused him to stumble into an exaggerated humanism.[5]

Pelagius would tolerate no fatal, insurmountable obstacle between God and man. Such a concession, he felt, would be fatal to the moral life of man as well as derogatory to his dignity. The humanism of Pelagius forced him to distort or deny the doctrines of divine grace and original sin when they proved incompatible with his views of human nature. A man who is supremely free, argued Pelagius, certainly has no need of divine grace in order to avoid sin. And if sin is the product of human freedom, then there can be no such thing as original sin, a sin in which the free choice of the individual has played no part.[6]

Strangely enough, the question of infant baptism proved to be the Pelagian stumbling block. It created a dilemma which finally destroyed them. The dilemma was based on a question. If there is no original sin, why is infant baptism necessary? The question left the Pelagians in a quandary. If they denied the necessity of infant baptism, they would undo the universal practice of the Christian world. If they admitted that it was necessary, they would acknowledge by implication the existence of original sin and destroy the logic of their own position. They tried various ways out of the problem but finally hit on one that was to become quite famous in centuries to come. They made a distinction between eternal life and the kingdom of God. Children, they said, could not enter the kingdom of heaven without baptism, but they could attain to eternal life. Baptism was necessary for the one but not the other.[7]

The Pelagian distinction relied on a somewhat novel interpretation of St. John's Gospel. In recording the discourse of Christ with Nicodemus, the Evangelist preserved those memorable words of our Lord: "Amen, amen I say to thee, unless a man be born again of water and the Spirit, he cannot enter into the kingdom of God" (John 3:5).*

The Pelagians pointed out that, according to Christ, baptism was necessary in order to enter the kingdom of heaven. He had not said that it was necessary for eternal life. Armed with this distinction, the Pelagians were now willing to admit the necessity of infant baptism. A child must be baptized if it is to enter the kingdom of God. Should it die unbaptized, however, its innocence would bring it to salvation and to eternal life. This distinction harmonized nicely with the total Pelagian construct. In their view man is capable of reaching God by the power of his own nature; and this would be eternal life. On the other hand, there was a more perfect reward, the kingdom, and he who would attain it must first undergo a sacramental initiation in baptism. The Pelagians did not deny that baptism could remove sin, but specified that it did so only when actual sin was present on the soul of the neophyte. Infants were baptized not to free them from sin but to render them precious in the sight of God, worthy of the kingdom he had prepared.[8]

AUGUSTINE VS. PELAGIANISM

The Pelagian view of unbaptized infants was born of necessity, and it was never among the cardinal doctrines of their heresy. Nevertheless, it opened a chink in their armor, and

* The scriptural passages in this book are quoted from *The Holy Bible,* Confraternity Edition. Copyright 1962, The Confraternity of Christian Doctrine.

Augustine hammered away at it in order to get at the heart of the heresy—the denial of original sin.

In retrospect Augustine's strategy seems quite clear. He would first prove that a child who dies unbaptized is eternally lost. With this idea clearly established, he could force the Pelagians to admit the existence of original sin. Nothing else could account for the eternal damnation of an otherwise innocent child. The major hurdle in Augustine's way, of course, was the Pelagian idea of "eternal life." He had to eliminate "eternal life" as a possible escape from damnation, and he was not even sure what the Pelagians meant by it. Was it the eternal life which Christ mentions so often in the New Testament? Or was it a totally new idea, a state of life midway between heaven and hell? He decided to take no chances; he would attack them on either score.

Assuming for the moment that the Pelagians were speaking of some halfway house between heaven and hell, Augustine set about tumbling it down. In his discourse on the last judgment Christ had said that all men would be placed either at the right hand of the judge or at his left. Those on the right hand of Christ would be welcomed into the kingdom of God, while those on his left would be condemned to the flames of hell. It was obvious, said Augustine, that a child who died unbaptized could find no place on the right hand of the judge. He must then take his place on the left with those condemned to eternal fire. There was no third alternative; no middle place into which an unbaptized child might escape.[9]

When he had eliminated one possible meaning of "eternal life" Augustine turned to the other. Perhaps the Pelagian eternal life was that spoken of by Christ in the Scriptures—a life that was clearly beyond the powers of men. In that case, argued Augustine, their position was even more untenable.

Christ had said that no one could have eternal life except by eating his flesh and by drinking his blood. This command extended not only to adults but to infants as well. However, since only a baptized person has the right to share in the body and blood of Christ, an unbaptized infant must necessarily be excluded from the holy table and hence from eternal life. In order to press his argument, Augustine made use of other texts of the Fourth Gospel in which Christ insisted on the necessity of believing in him in order to gain eternal life (John 3:18; 5:24). Baptized children are numbered among the believers, he added, by reason of their baptism, the sacrament of faith. Without this sacrament, however, there could be no faith, no eternal life.[10]

Once he had dealt with the idea of "eternal life," Augustine was ready to close his trap on the Pelagians. Children who die unbaptized are certainly excluded from the kingdom of God; and since eternal life for them is out of the question, nothing remains but eternal death. The Pelagians were now in a dilemma. Either they had to question the justice of God, or they had to admit the existence of original sin. God admittedly does not condemn the innocent. The condemnation of the unbaptized child demands an explanation, and the sin of Adam is the only explanation.[11]

Augustine had employed his formidable scriptural armament to exclude children from eternal life and from the kingdom of God. The question still remained: what precisely did eternity hold for them? Searching the Scriptures, Augustine could find but one answer—eternal death: and so in language that was largely scriptural he painted a chilling description of the future life of the unbaptized child. He must face the judgment of God, said Augustine; he is a vessel of wrath, a vessel of contumely, and the judgment of God is upon him. Baptism is the only thing that can deliver him from the kingdom of death and the power of the devil. If no one frees him from the grasp of the devil, what wonder is it that he must suffer in flames with Satan? There can be no doubt about the matter, the saint concludes, he must go into eternal fire with the devil.[12]

Augustine's opinion is severe, but its severity should not be exaggerated. When Augustine was accused of consigning infants and devils to one and the same torment, he denied it flatly. The wicked, he replied, will be punished according to the degree of their wickedness, and the punishment of children will be the slightest, the mildest of all. It will certainly be preferable to annihilation. At times Augustine not only tempered his language, but even seemed to waver about the idea itself. This paradox of vigor and vacillation was an element that would appear often in the history of this puzzling question.[13]

Reviewing this fifth-century debate, we may get the uneasy feeling that the antagonists have been miscast, with the villain's role falling to Augustine. Pelagius takes his stand on the side of the angels, advocating mercy and moderation, while Augustine relentlessly demands the supreme penalty. In this area of the controversy at any rate, present-day sympathies might lean toward Pelagius. Then too, Pelagius' opinion bears an undeniable resemblance to our modern views of limbo, and we have a natural tendency to favor the familiar. If we were men of another time and place, our sympathies might have gone to Augustine. As a matter of fact, this is precisely what did happen in the seventeenth and eighteenth centuries. Augustine was undeniably the hero of the moment, and the modern idea of limbo was rejected because it seemed Pelagian. Before we leave the Pelagian controversy it is imperative that we contrast the three points of view: Pelagius, Augustine, and limbo.

According to the Pelagians a child enters life in a state of innocence. Neither good nor bad at birth, he nonetheless has all the psychological equipment necessary to love God without a special divine assistance. God in his generosity has destined the child for an eternity that lies beyond the powers of his nature—the kingdom of heaven: and to attain it a sacramental initiation is necessary. Should the child die before he could be baptized, he would necessarily be excluded from the kingdom, but he would not be condemned to hell, for there was nothing evil in him deserving of so severe a sentence. Instead, he would spend his eternity in a place or state somewhere between heaven and hell; and this would be called eternal life.

There is an unmistakable similarity between the Pelagian "eternal life" and our modern limbo. In neither concept is the child judged worthy of heaven or of hell. Instead both consign him to some middle ground; there he knows neither the joys of heaven nor the torments of hell, but has a measure of happiness in keeping with his natural powers. So much for the points of contact between these two; the contrast between them is not immediately obvious, but it is crucial. In the Pelagian theory the child entered this life in a state of innocence and will spend his eternity in a state of innocence. In the limbo theory the child entered life as a sinner and will spend his eternity in a state of damnation. The limbo theologians insist that each of us is born with original sin on our souls. We are sinners not by choice but by heritage; nonetheless, we are "children of wrath." As a result, limbo is a state of damnation; that is, it is the consequence of a just sentence passed by God in punishment for sin. The Pelagians viewed "eternal life" as the natural complement to a state of innocence. Catholic theologians look upon limbo as an exile. Psychologically, this exile need have no effect on the child. He may or may not be aware that he has been banished from heaven; and in neither case need it disturb him. The fact of his exile remains, however, and it bears testimony to an idea that must be defended—original sin.

Augustine took a sterner view of the consequences of original sin than do modern theologians. A child who dies unbaptized is damned, said Augustine. A modern theologian would agree, but he would have his reservations about the sense of the word "damned." Essentially damnation means banishment from the presence of God: the modern theologian would deny that it need mean anything more. As a consequence he can quite logically conceive of a child under sentence of damnation who would neither suffer the torments of hell nor grieve over the loss of the beatific vision. The infant's exile from the presence of God would be enough to justify the use of the term "damnation." On the other hand, Augustine was unable to conceive a damnation that would not imply suffering of some sort. He was willing to grant for the sake of argument that children did spend their eternity in some place apart from the flames of hell; but even there, he argued, they could not be free of the greatest torment of the lost soul, its anguish over the loss of God. The Scriptures, however, seemed to forbid to grant them even this meager shelter from hell. Christ had indicated that there were but two possibilities at the final judgment. Man must stand either at the right hand of the judge or at his left. Those who were not at his right hand must leave him forever for the flames that had been prepared for the devil and his angels.

If we were to arrange schematically the ideas of Pelagius, Augustine, and limbo, they would look like this:

PELAGIANS

Unbaptized children
   are born in a
State of innocence
   and sentenced to
Neither Heaven nor Hell
   but rather
A Middle ground (eternal life)
   which is
A state of innocence,
   involving
Neither the pain of sense
   nor the pain of loss
But a measure of happiness.

LIMBO

Unbaptized children
   are born in a
State of original sin
   and sentenced to
Neither Heaven nor Hell
   but rather a
Middle ground (limbo)
   which is
A state of damnation,
   involving
Not the pain of sense
   nor grief over exile
But a measure of happiness.

AUGUSTINE

Unbaptized children
   are born in a
State of original sin
   and attain
Not to heaven, nor any middle ground
   but are rather sentenced to
Damnation
   in which they suffer
The pain of sense and the pain of loss.

AUGUSTINE AND THE CHURCH

Were Augustine's uncompromising views merely his personal opinions, or were they endorsed by the Church of his time? The question is important, for the teaching authority of the Church is the only secure anchor point in this matter. Down through the centuries the Church has led mankind through the treasure house of revealed truth, floodlighting one idea after another with her infallible authority. Much has been brought into focus; much still remains in the shadows. In the shadow areas theologians are free to speculate, constructing hypotheses, evolving theories. But however plausible their speculations, they remain hypothetical until the Church gives a decision. In a question as involved as ours we could easily get lost in a sea of speculation. Since the Church did enter the Pelagian controversy, it is important for us to see the results of her intervention.

THE BACKGROUND

Somewhere between the years 410 and 415 Pelagius left Rome for Africa in the company of his close friend, Celestius. They separated when they landed at Carthage. Celestius stayed in the city, while Pelagius went on to Palestine. Soon their simple seductive doctrine was spreading everywhere through the African Church. At first Augustine took no notice of it; and even when he did he was somewhat hesitant to attack Pelagius, who had acquired a remarkable reputation for sanctity. The Bishop of Carthage, however, had become alarmed; and at his request Augustine delivered a series of sermons at the Carthage Cathedral on the existence of original sin and the necessity of grace. Augustine's incisive mind quickly laid bare the whole Pelagian cancer; convinced of the danger, he threw all his energies into combating it in treatises, sermons, letters. The African bishops rallied around him to put an end to this new danger to their flocks.

Gathering at the episcopal sees of Carthage and Milevis, the bishops of Africa drafted two separate appeals to Pope Innocent asking a condemnation of the Pelagian error of "eternal life" without baptism.[14] To emphasize the importance of an early papal reply, Augustine and four other bishops sent a private letter to the pope. When the pope sanctioned the excommunication of the heretics, Augustine was overjoyed. The rescripts have come, he said in a sermon to the people of Carthage; the case is closed. Augustine's elation was short-lived; the pope was dead.[15]

Sensing a change in the political climate, Celestius hastened to Rome while Pelagius sent the pope a letter of submission and a proof of faith. Powerful friends in the Roman court arranged an audience and a hearing before Pope Zosimus. Celestius was able to convince the pope that the entire African affair had been no more than a clash of personalities.[16] Zosimus wrote at once to Africa informing the bishops there that he intended to dismiss the charges and remove the sanctions that had been levied against the two accused men. He added, however, that his final decision would be delayed for two months.[17] Unwilling to seem arbitrary, Zosimus had implicitly invited the African Church to clarify its position. Within weeks two hundred African bishops gathered at Carthage to formulate a reply. They reviewed the entire case against Pelagius and Celestius, examining again their alleged denials of original sin, divine grace, and the necessity of baptism. The accused were adjudged heterodox on every count. The council then formulated nine canons that summarized and condemned the Pelagian heresy; these they submitted to Pope Zosimus.

The decisions taken by the Council of Carthage are the clearest indication we have of the mind of the Church in this period. Two of its nine canons are relevant to our own problem. In the first of these the bishops condemn those who deny that a child must be baptized for the remission of original sin. In a second canon the council repudiates the notion of "eternal life" for unbaptized infants—the Pelagian corollary of denial of original sin.

"In like manner if anyone says that the words of
Our Lord 'There are many mansions in my Father's
House' must be understood in this sense, that there
exists in the kingdom of heaven or elsewhere an intermediate place where the children who die without
baptism live happily, while without baptism they
cannot enter the kingdom of heaven . . . let him be
anathema. Consequently what Catholic would hesitate to call him a co-heir of the devil who has not
merited to be called a co-heir with Christ? He who
is not at the right of Christ will surely be at his
left."[18]

These two decrees show clearly that the African bishops endorsed the main theme of Augustine's polemic while stopping
short of his total view of the problem of infant baptism. Neither
Pelagius nor Augustine had disputed the necessity of baptism.
The question at issue was: *why* must infants be baptized?
Original sin is the reason, said Augustine; and eternal damnation is the alternative. There is no such thing as original sin,
retorted the Pelagians. A child is baptized in order to prepare
him for life in the kingdom of God. Should he die unbaptized,
he forfeits not his soul but his heritage as a child of God.
Somewhere between heaven and hell there remains to him a
place of happiness consonant with his native goodness and
innocence.

Up to a point the bishops of Africa ranged themselves with
Augustine. Insisting first on the existence of original sin as the
reason for infant baptism, they went on to condemn the state
of happy innocence the Pelagians had promised the unbaptized child. Augustine's polemic, of course, had gone far beyond this point. Augustine had pursued the consequences of

original sin, concluding that damnation meant not only exile from God's presence but anguish over the loss, and the torment of fire. The Council of Carthage obviously agreed to the first of Augustine's conclusions. It seemed inclined to agree to the second and third when it spoke of any unbaptized child as a child of Satan and recalled the scriptural alternatives of heaven and hell at the final judgment. Officially, however, the council stopped short of Augustine's total view.

At first sight the decisions of Carthage might seem inimical to the modern notion of limbo. The historical context of these decisions, however, shows that they present no difficulty at all. True, limbo is a state or place of rest somewhere between heaven and hell, but it is a state of damnation. On the other hand, the "eternal life" of the Pelagians was a state of innocence that implied the denial of original sin; and it was the existence of original sin that concerned the bishops of Africa. All of this is plain to us today because the Holy See clarified the matter in 1784. That papal decision wrote finis to a debate that had generated a great deal of heat through two centuries. Limbo, it was claimed by the disputants, was incompatible with the decisions of Carthage. For the decrees of the African bishops had their roots in the age-old conviction that only heaven and hell will exist after the final judgment. The Pelagian controversy, it was said, only gave the bishops of Africa an opportunity to clarify and define this belief. Consequently, neither limbo nor any other "middle ground" is compatible with the decisions of the council. As we might suspect, only an authoritative decision by the Holy See could stop a discussion of this sort; the decision was given toward the end of the eighteenth century.

There is one obvious question still to be asked here. Why bother at all to study the decisions of the African bishops?

After all, the prelates assembled at Carthage represented only one segment of the Church and not the most important one at that. Their decisions would have an impact on the entire Church only if they were approved by the Roman pontiff. Augustine hints that this was done when he says that the Pelagian notion of an intermediate state was condemned by the "councils and by the Apostolic See." There is no conclusive evidence, however, that Pope Zosimus ever fully endorsed the decisions of Carthage. But the lack of pontifical approval does not mean that the decisions of Carthage are devoid of importance. They furnish us with a strong indication of the mind of the Church at the time. The bishops of Africa were not living in isolation. Historically they had always had the closest ties with Rome, echoing faithfully the cultural and religious developments of the older see. This bond between the two Churches explains in large measure the appeal of Africa to Rome in its condemnation of Pelagius. This same link between the two Churches placed Africa squarely in the mainstream of ecclesiastical thought. The decisions of Carthage were not isolated phenomena. We may fairly conclude that they represented more or less faithfully the mind of the Latin Church.

THE GREEK TRADITION

Fifteen years before Augustine entered the Pelagian controversy Gregory, the Bishop of Nyssa, was launching quite a different tradition in the Eastern half of the Christian world. Augustine consigned unbaptized infants to the fires of hell; Gregory dismissed the suggestion almost without comment. But then, Gregory was not immersed in a debate about the existence of original sin. As a matter of fact, the topic of original sin seemed to hold little interest for him; and in this perhaps he was typically a man of the East. Both the Eastern and Western halves of Christianity fell heir to the same traditions, of course; but historical exigencies and their own interests led them to develop different facets of Christian revelation.

Latin theologians were attracted by the subjective aspect of salvation, by the Christian's fight against sin and his practice of virtue. In this Augustine was representative of the West. Like all great souls he felt acutely the problem of good and evil. A prey to torment in his youth, he cast his lot with Manichaeism. This philosophy proposed a pessimistic view of the world, made it a battleground between good and evil personified by opposing divinities who left no opportunity for the exercise of human liberty. With his conversion to Christianity, Augustine unraveled the ancient riddle of good and evil; the doctrine of original sin was the clue to the puzzle. The depths of his personal conviction explain Augustine's waspish debate with Pelagius. Pelagius saw in man a being rich in energy, personally responsible for his good and evil actions, the arbiter of his temporal and eternal destiny. Man, retorted Augustine, is not healthy. He is fallen and in need of redemption. There is in his members a germ of evil that can be eliminated only by the aid of grace. Humanity is a mass infected by sin, a kingdom of Satan which Christ intends to transform into a kingdom of God by means of his Church. A man can escape the *massa damnata* only by the grace of God; and unless he does escape it, he is doomed to remain in the kingdom of Satan. Augustine's views of unbaptized infants are only the offshoot of his somewhat pessimistic anthropology.

The Greek theologians set divine revelation in a different perspective. They emphasized the objective value of the redemption and stressed the Incarnation of the Word of God that filled all mankind with divine power. The Greek apologetic for the Christian faith leaned heavily on the metaphysical content of the gospel. Stung by the scorn of the sophisticated Greeks, they set about proving that Christianity was superior to the Hellenistic philosophies that contemned it. Then too, their wrestling was not with the optimism of the Pelagians but with the fatalism of Mani and the Gnostics. Both the Manicheans and the Gnostics were deeply influenced by moral determinism; and in their struggle for human freedom the Eastern Christian writers were quick to stress the fact that sin has its origin in human liberty and not in some law of nature. This conviction of theirs was not a denial of original sin, since personal sin was the question under discussion. But it does explain why original sin, the sin of nature, should have remained somewhat in the shadows of their thinking. It explains, too, why one of their number should have been so emphatic in denying any positive punishment to children who died unbaptized.

The city of Nyssa has entirely disappeared from the maps of modern Turkey. It was only slightly less obscure in the year 371 when Gregory reluctantly agreed to be its bishop. He much preferred domestic bliss and the semi-retirement of the scholar to the burdens of administration, but his brother, Basil the Great, desperately needed episcopal allies in his struggle against the Arian heresy; and he was not beyond creating them. His relentless insistence brought Gregory to Nyssa; unfortunately it could not keep him there. Six years of office were ingloriously interrupted when Gregory's enemies trumped up a charge of malfeasance and had the unhappy bishop dismissed from his diocese.

Gregory spent most of his life in the shadow of his brother Basil; but then, so did most of his contemporaries. Scholar,

bishop, monk, but above all a man of action, Basil died when
less than fifty years of age; yet the history of the Eastern
Church resounds to his memory. Gregory had none of his
brother's extraordinary vitality. Basil easily outdistanced him
in almost every field. Still, of the two, Gregory had the more
penetrating intelligence. And it is this that has kept his writings alive for sixteen centuries.

Toward the end of his life Gregory wrote an essay "on the
early deaths of infants": he began it in a curiously poetic
way. "A human being," he said, "enters on the scene of life,
draws in the air, pays the tribute of a tear to nature," and then
dies. What becomes of him? Gregory asks. Is he punished? Or
is he admitted to the life of the blessed?

Gregory's answer to the first question is an emphatic "no."
The sufferings of the next life are the consequences of wickedness in this life. The saintliest of men and the tiniest of infants
have this at least in common—they are beyond punishment.
Gregory dismisses this whole question almost impatiently; it
shows that his problem lay elsewhere. Will such a child be admitted to the life of the blessed?[19]

Once again Gregory's answer is negative, but a strangely
qualified negative. There are men, Gregory remarks, who
would admit such children to the life of heaven. For his own
part he thinks their position unjust and unreasonable. Admitting the child to the life of the blessed would be unjust, he believes, because it would put him on a level with those who have
labored a lifetime to acquire virtue and overcome vice. Surely
it would be unfair to give the same reward to two men when
one has struggled for a lifetime and the other not at all.[20] But
even apart from this there is another more cogent reason for
excluding these children from the life of heaven; the child is
incapable of such a life. It would be wholly unreasonable to

introduce him "at once" to the life of the sage and the philosopher when his faculties are pulpy and unformed.[21]

Gregory elaborated on this curious qualification with an analogy. He notes that there is a gradual progression in our physical and intellectual development during our life on earth. An infant first feeds at the breast, and gradually grows stronger till at last it can take the nourishment of an adult. Gregory implies that a similar development may be expected in children who die prematurely. At first such a child will share in the life beyond the grave only so far as its embryonic faculties will permit. These faculties may be expected to develop, however, as they contemplate divine truth till finally they reach their full development. Then at last, to quote Gregory's phrase, "they will draw at will from that abundant supply of the truly existent [God] which is offered."[22]

One thing becomes clear as we read Gregory's essay: his reasoning applies equally well to baptized and unbaptized infants. To his way of thinking it would be no less unjust to admit a baptized child to the life of heaven than it would be to admit an unbaptized child. The one had struggled no harder or longer for virtue than the other. Nor would it be any less unreasonable, for the faculties of the two children are equally embryonic. The one is no more capable than the other of the life that Gregory envisions. Obviously, then, Gregory is writing on a much broader theme than Augustine had done. Augustine was concerned with the eternity of the unbaptized child. Gregory was puzzling over the child who died before it had the use of its faculties, whether it was baptized or unbaptized. The very breadth of this theme indicates the flaws in Gregory's theology of baptism and original sin.

Gregory seems to have underestimated the sacrament of baptism, judging it to be neither sufficient nor indispensable for the life of heaven.[23] While he certainly knew that baptism was a source of spiritual regeneration, he did not think that it was adequate to ensure a child's immediate entrance to the life of heaven. There must be a period of preparation during which the child's faculties would mature through contemplation. On the other hand, this same development would remove Gregory's objection to an unbaptized child sharing in the life of the blessed. The gradual flowering of its faculties would enable it to enter on the life of the sage and the saint.

Augustine would have been dumbfounded by these suggestions, because he had pondered so long on the consequences of original sin. Gregory acknowledged the existence of original sin, but he seems to have given little thought to its effect on the life to come. The whole idea of the sin of nature remained on the periphery of his theology; its relevance to his present problem seems never to have occurred to him.

There is more than a suggestion in this essay of Gregory's that he had fallen heir to a curious bit of theological bric-a-brac—a theory with the improbable name of the Apokatastasis. The creation of Origen, a theological giant of the early Eastern Church, the Apokatastasis meant "universal restoration." It implied the eventual salvation of every rational creature; all things had come forth from God; all things would find their way back to him. Those who have committed sin during their lives on earth will be subjected to fire after death, but it will be remedial as well as vindictive. The fires of hell are not eternal; the time will come when they will burn themselves out. All sinners will be saved; even the demons and Satan himself will emerge from the flames to be purified by the Word of God. When this has been achieved, Christ's second coming and the resurrection of men will follow and God will be all in all.

This idea is reminiscent of certain oriental philosophies. It jarred Christian tradition and ultimately fell into oblivion. Nonetheless it did leave an impression on Christian thought for many years. We seem, as we have noted, to find echoes of it in Gregory's essay. The crux of Origen's doctrine was, of course, the ultimate union of God and his creation, especially rational creation. Gregory envisioned infants who died prematurely as cut off from the life of the blessed by a psychological barrier. At the same time he conceived a law of growth that would permit them to surmount the barrier and ultimately enter upon the life for which they had been destined. The creature thus finds its way back to God.

From our modern point of view Gregory seems to be the man who suggests some of the right answers, but for all the wrong reasons. He denies that infants will suffer any punishment in the next life, but then he seems to equate punishment of sin with punishment of personal sin, ignoring the possible implications of original sin. He excludes infants from the life of the blessed, but his reasoning applies to baptized infants as well as to the unbaptized. He erects a psychological barrier between the children and their destiny and then sees the barrier being surmounted by the law of growth. In spite of these defects, Gregory's essay is an interesting one. There is nothing shallow or unoriginal about his intelligence, and it seems clear that he had an impact on the centuries of Greek thought that followed him. One idea in particular that he advanced in his essay was to survive him in the East, however; and this in quite a different form than he envisioned it. Children who die before baptism will neither be punished nor rewarded in the life to come.

Gregory, his brother Basil, and their close friend Gregory Nazianzen are known to history as the Cappadocians. To-

gether they were responsible for the renaissance of theology in
Asia Minor. Gregory Nazianzen had neither the vitality of
Basil nor the subtlety of his brother. He was an orator, one of
the most celebrated of his day. About the year 375 he delivered a sermon at Constantinople on the sacrament of baptism.[24] He discussed a problem that plagued the early Church
but which has little meaning for us today. Paradoxically
enough, he had to persuade his Christians to accept baptism.
Some of them wanted to postpone their reception of the sacrament as long as possible. These hard-headed Christians were
a bit too pragmatic. If they were to be baptized immediately,
they reasoned, they would have to struggle, perhaps for years,
to keep their innocence in a luxury-loving world. On the other
hand, if they delayed their baptism till the moment of death,
they would face their judge completely cleansed of sin. The
common sense of these practical men seemed to dictate delaying the reception of this remarkable sacrament until the last
possible moment. In his sermon at Constantinople, Gregory
bent all of his oratorical powers to removing the foundations
from under their complacency.

He pointed out the possibility of a premature and unexpected death forestalling their baptism forever. They would
then have to appear before God to stand trial on a double in-
dictment. Not only had they sinned, they had neglected the
God-given remedy for sin. Of course, Gregory added, not
everyone who neglected baptism would be judged equally
guilty by God. He then went on to distinguish three classes of
men. There were those who contemned the sacrament of baptism; and these would bear the heaviest responsibility. Then
there were the "practical" Christians who postponed their
baptism; theirs was a sin of stupidity rather than malice and
its consequences would be lighter. Finally there were those
who were prevented from receiving baptism by some circum-

stance beyond their control. Children who died unbaptized were of this sort. These would not be admitted to the glory of heaven, of course, but neither, said Gregory, would they be punished. "For not everyone who is not bad enough to be punished is good enough to be honored."[25]

The quotation we have just given is famous in the history of our whole question. At first glance it seems to catch up the essential idea of limbo—a life which is neither rewarded by heaven nor punished by hell. An argument for limbo could certainly be fashioned from Gregory's "proverb." But the reasoning that lies behind it might prove embarrassing to the man who employed it. Gregory had been lashing out at the pragmatists who delayed their reception of baptism. He insisted that the neglect of baptism was itself a sin calling for punishment. Of course, when the omission was inculpable, as it would be in the case of a child, it would go unpunished. The unbaptized child has done nothing that would warrant punishment; at the same time this personal innocence would not qualify him for the life of heaven. This seems to be the meaning of Gregory's proverb. If we conclude from this to Gregory's belief in the existence of some sort of limbo, we point up a flaw in his theology. Gregory, it would seem, had no clear idea of original sin, much less of its possible consequences in the life to come. If his proverb indicates a belief in a limbo of sorts, then his limbo stands four-square on an irrelevancy— the personal innocence of an unbaptized child. As we have already learned from Augustine, the doctrine of original sin is the real issue in any discussion of a child's eternity. Like his friend from Nyssa, Gregory Nazianzen seems to be giving acceptable answers for the wrong reasons. However that may be, the idea had been planted in Eastern thought; it would remain there.

We find the same idea bobbing to the surface in the writ-

ings of Cosmas Indicopleustes.[26] This remarkable surname
was the Greek way of describing the career of Cosmas "the
Indian voyager." Something of a sixth-century Marco Polo,
Cosmas was born at Alexandria in Egypt and destined for a
career in the business world. His mercantile adventures led
him across the Mediterranean, the Red Sea, and the Persian
gulf; and as he travelled he gathered information about lands
that lay far to the East. In his later years he retired to the
monastery of Raithu in the Sinai peninsula and wrote his extraordinary book, the *Christian Topography,* a work that
places him among the first Christian geographers. There was
little under the sun that Cosmas failed to discuss; and in-
evitably he examined the case of an infant dying before baptism. The answer he gives seems to reflect the thought of the
two Gregorys. Cosmas felt that children who die in the womb
stand in sort of a midway position in eternity, neither in glory
nor in suffering. They are refused a reward, he says, because
they have done nothing to warrant it; they are immune to
punishment because they have not had a chance even to taste
the good things of this life.

The same idea appears twice again in the sixth century in
two anonymous "manuals of doctrine."[27] In each case the
problem is briefly posed and briefly resolved. The first of
these anonymous authors frames his question a bit differently:
what distinction will there be in the resurrection between infants who die before baptism and those who die after it? The
author gives us only part of an answer. Those, he says, who
die after baptism will receive the benefits of the sacrament.
The implication is obvious: children who die unbaptized will
lose the reward attendant on the sacrament.

The other anonymous essay asks a similar question, but this
time the answer is a little more specific. Children who have

been baptized will enter the kingdom of heaven. Unbaptized children will not enter the kingdom, but neither will they be punished, for they have committed no sin.

A century later we hear the final word on the question from the near East before its long lapse into silence. In the seventh century the abbot of the monastery on Mount Sinai asked whether unbaptized infants would be among the damned in the life to come. The abbot answered that it would not be right to make children suffer for the sins of their parents. A premise of this sort demands an optimistic conclusion. Curiously enough, however, the abbot drew no conclusions.[28]

FULGENTIUS, AVITUS, AND GREGORY THE GREAT

While the mild views of the two Gregorys were making their way through the East, the opinion of Augustine was echoing in the West. Jerome, Augustine's irascible contemporary, seems to have taken it up. And we find clear indications of it in the sixth-century writings of Fulgentius, Avitus, and Gregory the Great.

Fulgentius was perhaps the most distinguished theologian of the sixth century, with a reputation for sanctity, eloquence, and learning. Although he lived almost a century later than Augustine, he was thoroughly devoted to his doctrine. If anything, he was even more explicit than his master in detailing a solution to our problem. Children who die without baptism, he says, will go into eternity to face the consequences of original sin, the everlasting torment of flame.[29]

We find a similar idea in the writings of Avitus,[30] but in a somewhat diverting context. Avitus, a distinguished bishop of Vienne in ancient Gaul, composed a treatise on chastity for his sister, a nun. In his essay he paints a gloomy picture of the trials of wedlock, and particularly of childbirth. In this context he introduces what must have seemed a crushing argument. A child, he says, may be snatched by death before it can be baptized. No longer a child of its mother, it becomes a child of perdition, begotten only for the flames of hell. Before judging Avitus too harshly we should recall that he was not only a bishop but a poet; and he was not beyond employing a certain poetic license.

Gregory I, the last of our sixth-century theologians, was one of the greatest of early popes. He was not a man of profound learning, not a philosopher, hardly even a theologian in the constructive sense of the term. He was a lawyer, monk, missionary and administrator par excellence. "In the strict account of God," he wrote, "it is but just that the stock of mortality, like an unfruitful tree, should preserve in the branches that bitterness which it drew from the root." Children who die without the sacrament were born in corruption; in the life to come they are "brought to torment."[31]

This same idea is carried into the seventh century by St. Isidore of Seville. Archbishop of Seville in Spain, and the last of the Fathers of the West, Isidore had a reputation of being the most learned man of his age. Neither original nor creative, he was primarily an encyclopedist; his writings preserved the sum of human knowledge available in his day. Tirelessly compiling the writings of the ancient Fathers, he bridged the gulf between the patristic era and the Middle Ages. His lack of originality and his dependence on the Fathers explain in large measure his views on the eternity of unbaptized children. He was simply giving voice to the ideas of the greatest of the Latin Fathers, Augustine. Unbaptized children, he wrote, will grieve in hell because of original sin.[32]

From what we have seen, it is clear that we would exaggerate if we were to speak of a tradition either in the Western or the Eastern Church. The ideas of Augustine and of the Gregorys moved through the centuries like smooth stones skipping across a pond, leaving traces of their passing. We also get the unmistakable impression of an echo growing less distinct as it moves away from its source. The successors of Augustine and of the Gregorys undoubtedly showed the influence of these masters. But the influence grows less marked and the ideas less distinct with the passing years. There are at least two explanations for this. The obvious one is the tempering effect that time has on strong opinions. The other is only slightly less apparent. The golden age of Christian literature had passed. Men no longer thought the great thoughts of the past, partly because the challenge was no longer there, partly because the lamp of learning was burning low in the Christian world. The empire had ensured a measure of peace and order in which men might ponder the truths of revelation. Now at last the empire was beginning to crumble, to yield yard by yard to the pressure of the barbarians in the West and the Mohammedans in the East. Thanks to men like Isidore of Seville, the literary wealth of an earlier age would not be lost. But for some time to come the scholars who survived would be forced to live off the capital heaped up in the past.

II

Scholastic Developments

THE PSEUDO-DIONYSIUS

Toward the close of the fifth century an unknown writer of the Eastern Church composed a number of treatises and letters that were destined to become famous. Perhaps to insulate his writings against the passing years, the author identified himself as a contemporary of the apostles. He claimed among other things to have seen the solar eclipse at the time of our Lord's crucifixion; he had also seen the "life-begetting, God-receiving body," i.e. of the Blessed Virgin. Whatever his real motive, the author succeeded in perpetrating an extraordinary hoax. In the centuries that followed his work was ascribed to Dionysius the Areopagite, the judge of Athens who was converted to Christianity by St. Paul.

We can well imagine the reverence with which these letters and essays were greeted by the men who read them. The author was supposedly a contemporary of the apostles, an eye-witness of their life and teaching. About the year 858 John Scotus Erigena, an Irish scholar, translated into Latin the Greek text of "Dionysius'" writings. The Irish theologian was competent in his own right, but his importance to Western theology was due to his translating the pseudo-Dionysius.[1]

Once introduced into the theological literature of the West, the works of Dionysius were readily accepted by the medieval theologians. The great masters of the university at Paris accepted his authority at face value and adopted many of his ideas. Among them was the notion of original sin as the privation, rather than the presence, of something. Original sin was seen not as concupiscence, not as corruption, but as the privation of the "original excellence conferred on our first parents." The idea may seem unremarkable enough now, but it was the footing on which men could erect a dialectical explanation of limbo.

History abounds in discoveries that were never exploited by the men who made them. In the world of the mind, men sometimes move to the threshold of an idea only to back away, unaware of how near they are to further finds. Anselm, the eleventh-century bishop of Canterbury, had this experience when he wrote his analysis of original sin. He developed the idea of Dionysius that original sin is privitive rather than positive in character.[2] He needed but a single logical step to conclude that the sin should be punished by a privation and by nothing more positive. He never took the step. When he came to discuss the consequences of original sin in the future life, he obediently echoed St. Augustine. There is no middle ground, he said, between salvation and damnation.[3]

PETER ABELARD

The man who finally broke with the five-century-old idea of St. Augustine was one quite accustomed to challenging the accepted way of doing things. His name was Peter Abelard (1079-1142).

Destined for an army career, Abelard chose a life of letters instead. He went to Paris and studied under William of Champeaux, one of the famous scholars of his day. The young man's violent temper, however, had him objecting vigorously to his professor and even attempting to set himself up as a rival teacher. Seven years later he actually succeeded in establishing himself as a master of the university, and students flocked to him from every country in Europe. At the height of his fame he abandoned his career to become entangled in one of the classic love stories of history: Heloise and Abelard.

This, then, was the brilliantly erratic scholar who felt no qualms about breaking with an ancient idea. Heir to Anselm's compelling presentation of original sin, he followed the idea to its logical conclusion, and made the punishment due to original sin a privitive rather than a positive thing. "In my opinion", he said, "[their] punishment consists in this alone, that they are in darkness, i.e. that they are deprived of the vision of the divine majesty without any hope of attaining it."[4]

Abelard took a great step away from his Latin predecessors, but it was single step, one of many that were later to follow. His view freed the children from any positive punishment that the fires of hell might inflict, but he seemed to go no further than this. Children, it seemed, must still suffer the grief of separation from God. He speaks of this mental anguish as a "torment of conscience"; and in this he seems a faithful echo of Augustine, who declared that exile from heaven was surely man's greatest suffering.

PETER LOMBARD

Abelard's idea might well have died with him had it not been for a rather ordinary man who wrote quite an extraordinary book, Peter Lombard, the Archbishop of Paris and the Master of the *Sentences*. Born in Italy about 1100, he was a student at Bologna, Rheims, and finally Paris. We learn from his own pupil, John of Cornwall, that he assiduously studied the works of Abelard, whose lectures he had probably followed about 1136. Between the years 1145 and 1151, when a professor at Notre Dame in Paris, he composed his book of *Sentences*. And it is this theological work that gave him a unique place in the theology of the Middle Ages. Divided into four books, the *Liber Sententiarum* covers the whole body of theological doctrine and welds it into a systematized unity. The book is hardly more than a compilation; scarcely ten lines have been found to be completely original; but Peter made no secret of this. His purpose was to write a sort of corpus that would save the time of searching through many volumes. Aside from this, the book has undoubted merit. He made a successful effort to reconcile the roles of reason and authority in theology, a point that was causing no end of difficulty in the twelfth century. Besides, his attempted solutions of so many problems aroused the students' curiosity and led their professors to write endless commentaries.

The book of *Sentences* was not an immediate success, but when recognition did come it was overwhelming. From the twelfth to the sixteenth century it was the textbook in university courses; each future doctor of theology was required to comment on it for two years. Thomas Aquinas, Bonaventure, Alexander of Hales and Duns Scotus were some of the great theologians who cut their teeth on the *Sentences* of Peter Lombard. When Lombard agreed, then, with Abelard that unbaptized infants suffer only "darkness" in the world to come, the idea spread through the universities of Europe.[5]

HONORIUS OF AUTUN

Before we leave the twelfth century, we might ask ourselves to what extent Abelard's idea had penetrated from the university hall into the thinking of the faithful. Theologians might speculate on the consequences of original sin without having their ideas filter down to the laity. The question is not without significance. If there was a widespread conviction among the faithful, then we may presume that it reflected an equally widespread opinion among the theologians of the time. We can sometimes gain an insight into the mind of the faithful by studying the catechetical literature with which they are instructed, by reading the sermons that they heard. There is one book dating from the twelfth century that answers this description—the *Elucidarium* of Honorius of Autun, that summary of Christian doctrine on which we touched briefly in our Introduction. Originally written in Latin, the book was translated into French and then into German. From the number of manuscripts that have survived (sixty in France alone), we know that it was very widely used from the twelfth to the fifteenth century.[6] It served a double purpose. It was a book of instruction for clerics and religious; and it provided a handy reference book for priests in their work with their people. It was probably used to help with the instruction of children too. Because it was so widely used over a period of four centuries, it gives us some hint of what the ordinary faithful thought of the problem of unbaptized infants in the life to come.

In Honorius' chapter on the "future life" we are told that there are two hells ("infernos"), an upper and a lower.[7] The upper hell is situated in the lowest regions of our own world; and it is a place of punishment, of great cold and of stifling heat, of hunger and thirst, of fear and terror. The lower hell is a spiritual place, where we find an inextinguishable fire: and here we find nine different punishments corresponding to the particular malice of the sinner: fire, cold, serpents and dragons, blows, etc. The just who lived before the coming of Christ waited for the Messias in the upper hell in a place where they could look down upon the torments of the damned. To the damned beneath them they appeared to be in paradise; and hence we find Dives pleading with Lazarus for a drop of water to cool his tongue. Nevertheless, these exiles felt themselves in hell because of their separation from the kingdom of God. This "darkness," however, was their only punishment, a punishment shared by children who died without baptism.[8]

Medieval ideas about unbaptized infants had moved a long way from Augustine by the end of the twelfth century, thanks to Dionysius, Anselm and Abelard. They were destined to evolve dramatically in the thirteenth century. We find, perhaps, the clearest picture of this evolution in Dante as he reflects the masters of the thirteenth, the "greatest of centuries."

DANTE

Thomas Aquinas himself remarks on the metaphor's power to communicate the truth; Dante is a remarkable illustration of the truth of Thomas' remark.[9] Aquinas had reached the height of his fame before Dante was born; he died before Dante reached his tenth birthday; yet, as Benedict XV remarked in his encyclical on Dante, there is a kinship between the poet and the saint. For Dante had immersed himself in the writings of the medieval masters, Thomas above all; and his *Divine Comedy* is in its own way as much a *Summa* as the great work of Thomas.

Dante's theology is that of the great medieval masters, but his imagery is that of the people. As we have said, we find the inspiration for his Inferno in the *Elucidarium*. As Dante envisioned it in his allegory, the realm of the damned was a vast circular chasm that led by slow degrees to the pit of hell. Each of the nine stages in the descent corresponded to some state of malice in the human soul. Treason, for instance, buried a man in the pit of hell: treason to friends, kinsmen, countrymen, benefactors. Here then we find Judas who betrayed Christ, Brutus who betrayed Caesar, and Satan who betrayed God. Above these, in a place of lesser torments, are those who led others into sin for their own profit or advantage. And so the pattern goes—each crime finds its proper punishment.

In recounting his underworld journey, Dante begins by saying that Virgil "ushered me into the topmost ring that circles the abyss. But in this ring, so far as one could judge, there were no cries of woe but only sighs." Standing as it does on the shore of the "lip of woe," limbo doesn't seem too unpleasant a place. Dante imagined an imposing citadel, with seven circling walls, a lovely river, a "meadow, fresh and green, a high open place suffused with light." The picture strikes us as fanciful, and indeed it is, but it is important to recall Aquinas' remark that metaphor and allegory may be used to teach a spiritual truth.[10]

In his own inspired fashion Dante was following the lead of the theologians who had broken away from the opinion of Augustine; more precisely, he was in the tradition of Thomas Aquinas, who not only placed children beyond the reach of torment but envisioned them enjoying a measure of real happiness. The keynote of Dante's halfway world, however, seems to have been tranquillity. The lives of these children entailed neither great sorrow nor real joy. Their surroundings were pleasant enough, but there was about them an air of regret for the lost kingdom of God. In this vision, a dramatic refinement of the idea of limbo in the *Elucidarium,* Dante, as we shall see, followed Bonaventure rather than Aquinas.

THOMAS AQUINAS

In the year 1251 an immense young friar was appointed sub-regent of the Dominican Studium in Paris. Thomas was his name; and the Italian Counts of Aquino were his ancestors. He is known to history as Thomas Aquinas, saint and doctor of the Church. Thomas' duties as sub-regent were largely pedagogical and heavily demanding. His lectures on the *Sentences* of Peter Lombard necessarily ranged over the whole of philosophy and theology. So far as we know, it was in the fourth book of these *Sentences* that Thomas first encountered the problem that is posed by the death of an unbaptized child. Typically enough, Peter had done no more than indicate what he considered to be the solution of the problem; and Thomas in his commentary elaborated extensively on the Lombard's theme. It was somewhat typical of Thomas, too, that he was not entirely satisfied with his own early analysis of the question; and over the years he recast some of his earlier ideas. In the end he had pretty well shaped the idea to which Dante gave poetic expression in the *Divine Comedy*.

Thomas' own infernal geography is a good deal less complicated than Dante's but scarcely less imaginative. Thomas envisioned a fourfold inferno that embraced the damned, the just of the Old Testament, the Church suffering and unbaptized children. The deepest regions of hell, said Thomas, are reserved for those who are guilty of serious personal sin. They are confined there in darkness to be tormented eternally by the pain of sense. Above this inferno of the damned Thomas placed the limbo of children. Here Thomas envisioned a double darkness, a metaphor that denoted the lack of divine grace and the privation of the beatific vision. Purgatory stood on a higher level still; and above it could be found the limbo of the Fathers. Here the just of the Old Testament had awaited the coming of Christ.[11]

In sketching his infernal topography, Thomas followed the lead of the medieval scholastics. Naive as they may appear, perhaps, to the modern mind, these men had not simply swallowed whole the legends of simple folk. They had taken their position at the apparent command of cold logic. Reason told them that not even a disembodied spirit could be everywhere; it must be somewhere; and hence their attempts to localize it. Their sense of justice told them that there should be some proportion between the soul's worth and the place assigned it by God for eternity. These two convictions explain their attempt to visualize the geography of the world to come. They had plenty of precedent for their speculations too. Christian writers of nearly a thousand years before had distinguished an upper and lower hell in which the damned and the just of the Old Testament awaited the coming of Christ and the final judgment.[12] As the medieval theologians refined their speculations on the future life, they made a more elaborate geographical division in order to accommodate them. Albert the Great even coined a name for these regions that stood on the borders of hell: Limbo.[13]

Two of Thomas' infernal departments are of special interest to us, the hell of the damned and the limbo of children. Although Thomas placed unbaptized children on the borders of hell itself, he denied emphatically that they suffered the torments of the damned. To appreciate his denial we should recall that there is a double element in every mortal sin committed by the damned: a turning away from God and a turning to some created good in place of God. The first is punished in hell by eternal separation from God; this is the essential sanction of hell, and by far its greatest torment. In their desperation the damned hate the God they were made to love; they are engulfed in a endless flight from the thing they instinctively crave. So exquisite is their anguish that some have identified it with the "fires of hell." This is incorrect. The grief of the damned finds its source within them. There is another torment in hell caused by something quite apart from the person himself. This external agent of torment is the fire of which the Scriptures speak; for want of a better term, theologians have called it the pain of sense. There is a supreme irony in the existence of this material agent of torment. The damned had turned from God to embrace his creation; now creation torments them for the dishonor they have done their creator.

According to Thomas, the children of limbo linger in a metaphorical darkness. They lack divine grace and they have lost the vision of God, but they do not suffer the anguish of the damned. Thomas rests his case on an analysis of sin and sanction, of crime and punishment.

The *raison d'être* for the pain of sense is lacking in the case of children. There has been no abuse of God's creation, no turning aside from God to his creatures. Abuse creation, Thomas remarks, and it will abuse you. If we eat or drink too much, we become sick. Not only has the food failed to give us strength, it has positively injured us. It is fitting, then, that those who abuse creation should be punished by creation or its representative, the fire of hell. In the case of children, however, there has been no abuse of creation, no turning aside from creator to creature. And consequently there is no reason why they should suffer the retaliation of creation.[14]

The one sin of these children is theirs by heritage, not by choice. Original sin is not a positive fault but rather a privation. These children are born without the divine grace that should have been their inheritance from Adam. God kindled the fires of divine life; had Adam kept it alive, it would have been passed from generation to generation till the earth was aflame with it. But Adam sinned; and the fire died. Men are born deprived of divine life; and this privation is original sin. Since the punishment must fit the crime, Thomas argued that a positive punishment would be unreasonable for something that was not a positive fault, but only a privation.[15]

It is true, he admitted, that even children are inclined to moral disorder because of original sin. We are not punished, however, for our inclinations but only for our actions. We may feel inclined to strangle the neighborhood nuisance; but so long as we resist the temptation, there can be no retribution. On this score, then, there is no ground for the pain of sense in children.[16]

Perhaps Thomas' most interesting argument against the pain of sense is to be found in his analysis of punishment. Children cannot be punished by the pain of sense, Thomas insisted, because the punishment would be unreasonable. Briefly, his argument is this. If a man's powers are to be deprived of their well-being by the pain of sense, this punishment must bear some relation to a fault in the person who used those powers. In the case of an infant such a relation cannot be established. And therefore the punishment would be unreasonable. Since this line of reasoning is not immediately obvious, we might explain it a bit further.[17]

The crux of Thomas' argument seems to be the relation that exists between a person and his natural faculties: mind, will, touch, taste, and so forth. A person is a responsible agent; as such, he acts through these channels opened up by his nature. As a result, there is an intimate and necessary relation between the person and these faculties. He is entirely responsible for their activities. A man cannot claim that his hand shot some innocent by-stander in cold blood, but that he himself had nothing to do with it. He may protest this to the moment he is strapped into the electric chair, but society will ignore him. Society sees an immediate relation between this man and his faculties. The electricity that hums through the chair in the death chamber is not only thoroughly disagreeable and wholly unwelcome, but as it destroys the natural faculties of the man, it reaches beyond them to the person who employed them in a criminal way.

In the case of a fault that cannot be traced to the person we are on totally different ground. Let us say that it is a purely hereditary fault, one that the person acquired by birth and not by choice. We might have thought such a thing impossible, had it not been for divine revelation. Our faith, however, teaches us that there is such a thing as original sin. It is a real deviation from the divine economy, and consequently a sin. It is something peculiar to each of us; and yet it is not a personal fault. The fact that each of us is born without the divine grace that should be ours is an abomination in the sight of God. It makes us "children of wrath," to employ the scriptural phrase. And since it is a real sin, it should be punished. But what shall the sanction be?

We have seen that the natural faculties of a man may be stripped of their integrity in punishment for a personal sin because of the immediate relation which these faculties bear to the person who misuses them. On the other hand, no such relation can be established in the case of a child. The fault is inherent in the nature, it cannot be traced to the person. Hence the child's integrity cannot reasonably be disturbed in punishment.

Thomas, it is clear, ruled out the pain of sense as a punishment for original sin. But the pain of sense is not the greatest torment of the damned. By divine decree the children in limbo are eternally exiled from the vision of God. Do they chafe under their misfortune? Do they rebel against the providence that banished them? St. Thomas had a more difficult problem here than he did in dealing with the pain of sense. Augustine and John Chrysostom alike had insisted that the loss of heaven was a far greater torment than the fire of hell. And surely this loss would be felt far more keenly by one who was innocent of any personal guilt! How, then, could children help resenting their exile, and the providence that had decreed it? Thomas gave two answers to the question over a period of some ten years; and in doing so he shifted ground remarkably.

In the year 1255 Thomas completed his commentary on the *Sentences* of Peter Lombard. At that time he remarked that no one regrets the lack of something which he is totally unequipped to have. A man may regret the loss of his home, his family, his good name; but no reasonable man permits himself to be distressed over his inability to fly like a swallow. The analogy holds good in the case of the child in limbo. The child will know that he was meant for the beatific vision; he will know, too, why he lost his chance to enjoy it, but it won't distress him. He will see too clearly that he has no natural ability to enjoy the beatific vision. The intuitive vision of the divine nature is farther beyond his reach than flying is beyond the corner butcher's. It is conceivable, of course, that there are people who get upset over their inability to fly like birds; but such people are confined to institutions. We don't find them in the reasonable world of limbo.[18]

Some ten years later St. Thomas had a second thought on this problem.[19] Children, he finally decided, will not be disturbed over their loss simply because they will not know what they have lost. They will go through eternity unaware of their supernatural destiny, never dreaming of the sin that put it beyond their reach. They will, of course, reason to the fact that they were meant to possess God. Since they have not the knowledge of faith, they will never guess the divine decree that would admit man to the vision of God; and what they don't know won't hurt them. They will spend eternity contemplating God so far as their nature permits, never dreaming that they were destined for something immeasurably more glorious.

St. Thomas had shown that children were not unhappy in limbo. Still another question remained: were the children happy? The difference between these two states of mind is not especially subtle. We may ask our neighbor how he is feeling and have him reply that at least his ulcer isn't bothering him. The answer tells us little aside from the absence of an obvious torment; it is one thing not to be unhappy, and quite another to be happy. Did the green meadow and glistening river of Dante's poem speak of a natural happiness? Most theologians would say that the question is to some extent an unreal one. Man was meant to spend his eternity enjoying the vision of God. That is the final purpose of our lives; in it we find our fulfillment or "beatitude," as theologians would say. Deprived of this fulfillment, could any human being find real happiness?

St. Thomas says that the children of limbo can be happy, in spite of their exclusion from heaven. It is true that they are separated from God insofar as they do not enjoy the beatific vision, but they are united to God by their native ability to know and to love him; and in this they find their happiness.

The question of human happiness has troubled man since

he first began to think. Human genius has exhausted itself in trying to determine what it is that will give man the happiness he wants. The fact is that man can be satisfied only by what is absolutely good, something without the slightest limitation to disillusion him. This is but another way of saying that man can be satisfied by nothing less than God himself.

There is an obvious difficulty in this business of finding our ultimate happiness in the possession of God. The human mind is naturally incapable of seeing God as he is. Now and again it can glimpse something of his perfection; it cannot possibly encompass the divine being itself. For this to be possible, there would have to be an intimate union of God and the human mind, a permanent, wholly satisfying union; but a union of that sort is completely beyond the natural powers of man. He is condemned by what he is to quarry his knowledge from the granite of creation by the slow process of abstraction and reasoning. This painful process never lets him come face to face with his creator as he is, but only as he is found reflected in the world he made. At least, this would have been the situation, had it not been for God's decision to admit man to a destiny beyond his nature.

When God created Adam he decreed that the human family was to find its ultimate happiness in nothing less than the vision of God as he is in himself. He planted the seeds of a new life in his creature—the life of grace. Henceforth, then, the human mind would have the germ of a new way of knowing— a vision beyond the powers of men. At death, if the life were preserved, a second gift would be given—the perfect complement of the first. It would be called the light of glory.

Some faint analogy of this can, perhaps, be drawn from the world we know. It is as if, until this moment, the human mind had been like a man seated on a mountaintop before sunrise.

He was poised at the roof of the world; creation lay at his feet, but he was blind to it. Not that he lacked the faculty of sight, but he sat in darkness. The light of glory is like the sun rising over the world; it climbs the mountaintops and plunges into the valleys, splashing the world with color, form, dimension, opening to human eyes all the beauty of creation.

Once God had decreed that man was made for this intimate union with the divine, there could be but one goal for the human race, the vision of God. Failing this goal, they must drift forever in the world of reflection, content with the shadows of God's perfections rather than with the reality. This is the condition in which unbaptized children find themselves in limbo. The vision of God is utterly beyond them. Unaware of what they have lost, Thomas says, they find God in his creation, and knowing him, they love him; and in their knowledge and love of God they find their happiness.[20]

THE OTHER SCHOLASTICS

How representative were the opinions of St. Thomas? Was he speaking for himself, or did he voice the views of the other Schoolmen? Thomas often walked alone, far ahead of the men of the time, but his views of an infant in eternity were the views of his age. The unique position that the *Sentences* of Peter Lombard held in the universities served to spread his own mild views all through Europe. We can find no theologian of the thirteenth century who thought that infants suffered the pain of sense in punishment for original sin. There seemed to be widespread agreement, too, that infants would suffer no distress over their separation from the kingdom of God.[21] Theologians did differ widely in assigning reasons for this, however. As we saw, Thomas used two quite different arguments. In

1255 he said that children are aware of their lost destiny but feel no regret. In 1265 he said they feel no regret because they have no idea of what they have lost. Durandus of St. Porcain agreed.[22] Saint Bonaventure, however, had quite a different reason to offer. Children in limbo, he said, enjoy a perfect balance between their knowledge and their desires, thanks to the good offices of their creator. Since grief would imply a lack of balance, it can have no part in the lives of these children. These children stand midway between the blessed and the damned, and so they share something of each state of life. Like the damned they are exiles from heaven; like the blessed, they know no grief.[23]

The English Franciscan Richard of Middleton touched close to the heart of the matter when he wrote that grief is not essential to the pain of loss. Essentially this punishment consists in exile from the presence of God. If this loss is seen as the result of one's personal faults, grief results. Since children are innocent of any personal fault, they feel no regrets.[24] Duns Scotus, another remarkable Franciscan, was a bit more subtle in his approach to the problem. Children, he said, die in a state of personal innocence; by divine decree they will remain so for eternity. Were they to grieve over their loss of heaven, they would lose their innocence either by murmuring against God or by sinking into despair. This is clearly impossible. Since they died without personal fault they will remain so for eternity. Therefore there can be no unhappiness among them over what they are or what they have lost.[25]

According to Scotus, there can be no unhappiness of any sort in limbo. Grief, he remarks, is a greater punishment than the pain of sense, because it attacks a higher faculty, the human will. Since children are spared the pain of sense, they must logically be free of any unhappiness. It would be absurd to suppose that they were spared the lighter punishment and left to bear the heavier.[26]

The greatest theologians of the Middle Ages agreed that children in limbo would suffer no distress. They parted company, however, when they discussed the question of happiness. Some thought that the children lived a somewhat static existence, their emotions and appetites so perfectly balanced that they felt neither sadness nor joy. Divine justice, so Bonaventure said, established them in an unchanging state of knowledge and love which knew neither progress nor retrogression, sadness nor joy.[27]

On the other hand a reputable group of Schoolmen thought that those in limbo enjoyed an unusual measure of happiness; among these we find Thomas Aquinas, Scotus, Durandus, Dionysius the Carthusian, Peter of Tarentaise (later Pope Innocent V), and Richard of Middleton.[28]

Actually the Scholastics spend little time speculating on the psychological life of those in limbo. Bonaventure, as we have seen, thought that they would never experience the disorderly movements consequent on an imbalance between knowledge and desire. Scotus was even more optimistic. These children, he said, will have a far more excellent knowledge of the world about them than we could possibly have in this world. For their intellects will be hindered neither by suffering, nor by the weakness of corruptible flesh, nor by the inordinate movements of concupiscence. St. Thomas Aquinas would add his qualified assent to these opinions. Those in limbo will have a perfect knowledge of the natural world, he said; but they will not have the knowledge of faith. Certain facts will remain forever beyond their intellectual horizons. They could not reason to the existence of the triune God. Nor could they ascertain the fact of their being destined to the intuitive vision of God. But the world that meets their senses, the invisible world of ideas that it suggests, will lie open to them.

What will be the physical state of those in limbo after the resurrection? Scotus and Bonaventure raised the question; in answering it, they agreed that the bodies of those in limbo would be immune to suffering. A divine decree and not the gift of impassibility would explain the immunity. This is another way of saying that the bodies of these children will not share the reward that is the special privilege of the blessed in heaven. By divine concession the glorified bodies of the saints are endowed with a gift that puts them beyond suffering. Those in limbo do not have this gift, but God's providence sees that nothing hurts or distresses them. They could pass through flames unharmed, says Bonaventure.[29]

As we glance back along the road down which we have come, we find that the idea of limbo was slow in entering the Western world. Anselm of Canterbury pointed the way with his analysis of the privitive character of original sin. Abelard drew the logical conclusion when he suggested that the punishment too was privitive rather than positive. It remained for Peter Lombard to introduce the idea into the lecture halls of Europe by means of his *Sentences*. The twelfth-century Scholastics had taken a giant step away from Augustine; but their limbo was still a primitive thing. Peering into this halfway world, they could see nothing but darkness; and "darkness" became a catchword for the future life of infants. The restless minds of the great Scholastics insisted on probing further into the problem. They were in fair agreement that those in limbo suffered neither fire nor grief over the loss of heaven. Further than that they would not go without some difference of opinion. Some thought the children would know neither joy nor sorrow, their minds and emotions in perfect balance. Thomas thought differently and so did others. There was no reason, they believed, why these children should not share in God's goodness through the natural powers they possessed. Their powers of intellection and volition are not only unimpaired, they are unhampered by concupiscence or fatigue.

THE CHURCH

Nearly a thousand years lie between Augustine and the great Scholastics, and an even greater gulf separates their thought. Theologians had taken immense strides away from Augustine. Did the Church's teaching authority keep pace with them, or did she leave them free to speculate? There are several instances in which the Church voiced her mind in the matter. Innocent III was the first to speak.

One of history's most remarkable Popes, Innocent reigned at a time when Church and state were bound together in something called Christendom. This remarkable union of the spiritual and temporal worlds placed Pope Innocent at the head of Europe.

Fifty years before St. Thomas arrived in Paris, Pope Innocent wrote a letter to the Archbishop of Arles, replying to a difficulty that had been proposed. In the course of his letter Innocent spoke of the punishment appropriate to actual and to original sin. Actual sin, said Innocent, is punished by the endless torment of hell; but original sin is punished by the loss of the vision of God.[30]

This letter was written in 1201 at a time when theologians were moving en masse away from the ancient theory of hellfire for unbaptized infants. At first glance, it would seem that Innocent's letter endorsed their opinion; theologians, however, are prone to second glances at papal documents. Over the centuries they have noted several points that are worth mentioning. In the first place Innocent III was not exercising his full magisterial power in this letter. He was answering the special difficulty of a particular bishop. Secondly, the letter would not have ended all discussion, even if the pope were speaking with the fullness of his authority. If we examine the pope's reply carefully, we find that he was indicating the punishment that was appropriate to the sins in question; he did not say that the appropriate or proper punishment was the only punishment. By saying that the pain of sense was proper to actual sin, he surely had no intention of excluding the pain of loss.

This distinction may seem a bit of theological pedantry, but history proves the contrary. This very question was discussed by Albert the Great; and Albert's solution disagrees with Innocent. Albert denied that children suffered the pain of sense; but he denied that the loss of the beatific vision was the punishment appropriate to original sin.[31] Innocent's letter does little to endorse the scholastic speculations on limbo, but it is important for another reason. It is the first time that the teaching authority of the Church has taken cognizance of the pain of loss and the pain of sense as two very distinct torments of the damned. And this itself is an important part of the whole problem of unbaptized children. Little enough, we may think, from a papal pronouncement. But at least it is one more anchor point in a discussion that has all too few of them.

The Church stepped center stage in this discussion once more in the thirteenth century during the Council of Lyons.

THE SECOND COUNCIL OF LYONS (1274)

One of the problems that troubled the Middle Ages concerned the moment at which a departed soul would receive its reward or punishment. In the very early days of the Church some writers had thought that the execution of God's judgment would be deferred until the second coming of Christ at the end of time. St. Justin Martyr, for instance, believed that both the wicked and the good would have to await the final judgment, the good in a pleasant place, the wicked in an unpleasant one. Only after Christ's definitive sentence would the sinners be delivered to eternal flames and the just to immortality. The millennium was a variation of this same ancient theme. Essentially it meant that Christ at the end of time would establish a kingdom on earth where the just would reign gloriously with him for a thousand years, enjoying the highest spiritual and material blessings. At the end of this millennium the just would be introduced to the vision of God. This idea of a delayed reward hung on into the Middle Ages. In three of his sermons Pope John XXII (1249-1334) expressed the opinion that the vision of God as well as the essential punishment of the damned would be deferred until the end of the world. Two councils of the Church laid the question to rest: the Second Council of Lyons and the Council of Florence.

The Second Council of Lyons was called in 1274 in hopes of healing the Eastern Schism. Political circumstances seemed opportune for healing the breach between the East and the West. The Byzantine Emperor Michael VIII feared the ambition of Charles of Anjou, the King of Naples and Sicily. In the hope that Rome might hold Anjou in check, Michael approached the Papacy, offering to reunite the two Churches; he would make a profession of faith and submit to the authority of Rome. Rome welcomed the offer somewhat naively; since it was a purely political move on Michael's part, it was doomed to fail. Nonetheless the profession of faith was made and formally accepted by the Council of Lyons. Among the doctrines thus defined by the council we find the following:

"However, the souls of those who die in mortal sin, or with original sin alone, shortly go down to hell, to be punished with different punishments, however."[32]

In 1439 in another unsuccessful attempt at reuniting the Greek and Latin Churches, the Council of Florence repeated these words almost verbatim.[33]

These two councils clearly are defining the fact of retribution for sin shortly after death. Do they also intend to define the existence of limbo as we have seen it explained by the medieval theologians? It would seem not. Within a few centuries we will find a whole group of theologians arguing that the words of Lyons and Florence are in fact a rejection of limbo and a canonization of the opinion of St. Augustine. Augustine, as we saw, taught that children would be punished in hell but with the mildest of all punishments. In the course of history we will encounter at least four interpretations of Michael's profession of faith: (1) Lyons and Florence teach that there are those who actually do die guilty of nothing but original sin; (2) Lyons and Florence do not teach that there are those who actually die in original sin alone; they teach what will happen should someone die in original sin; (3) the councils are canonizing the limbo of the medieval theologians; (4) the councils are endorsing the opinion of St. Augustine.

In 1321 Pope John XXII wrote a letter to the Armenian Church in which he stated:

"The Roman Church teaches . . . that the souls of those who die in mortal sin, or with original sin alone, shortly go down to hell to be punished in different places and with different punishments."[34]

It is not clear whether John's letter was dogmatic or disciplinary; hence its precise theological value is uncertain. Moreover, it falls prey to the same division of opinion we have seen above.

Just about this time we are ready to hurry back to the little island of agreement from which we launched forth. The waters are still too deep and too unsettled for the Church to wish to give a clear decision on the matter. As a result, we leave the period of the great scholastic theologians without having seen any extensive endorsement of their work by the teaching authority of the Church. The Church seemed content to let the years of discussion chip away at the problem till finally the truth should stand clear and free. She struck at error when it threatened in the fourth century and again in the Middle Ages. She will do so again in a later age. Save for this the age-old process of uncovering the truth was left to go on unimpeded, unaided.

III

The Age of the Reform and After

The scholastic synthesis of philosophy and theology was a bold attempt to weave into a pattern all that was known of God and man. The resulting "world view" was an achievement that has seldom been equalled in human thought. Dante's *Divine Comedy* owes much of its stature to the *Weltanschauung* of the Middle Ages. In full vigor in the thirteenth century, Scholasticism grew old in the fourteenth century and decayed in the hundred years that followed. The medieval monument to human thought was overgrown by a tangle of verbiage and lost in the forest of nominalism. This was the scholastic ruin that Luther despised and the Renaissance mocked as they turned back to antiquity in their quite different quests for truth. There were others, however, who caught a glimpse of greatness in the ruins of Scholasticism. Slowly, painfully they began to strip away the overgrowth and uncover the giant structure that lay beneath. Here they found weapons with which to engage in a new intellectual apostolate, one that sought to win back the men of the Renaissance and construct a Christian humanism. For a brief period of time it seemed as though they would succeed; the science of divine truth seemed to be entering on a second spring. Then history took an unfortunate turn, and theology began to bury its head in the sand. Jansenism cursed the Renaissance and fled back to Augustine, renouncing the centuries that intervened. The Catholic world was split on a controversy that should never have been. Some of the Church's finest moments have been found in the response of great men to a great challenge. Jansenism was not so much a challenge as a retreat, and there were no great men to stem the rout. The theological renaissance of the sixteenth century bloomed briefly, and then died under the chill wind of Jansenism. But in that brief period the scholastic notion of limbo reached its highest development.

AMBROSE POLITI: THE NEW EARTH

Ambrose Politi, the distinguished Dominican theologian of the Council of Trent, was the first modern theologian to devote an entire monograph to the problem of unbaptized infants.[1] His little book is memorable for several of its suggestions. Politi denied, of course, that original sin would be punished by the sufferings of hell. Children who bore this sin into eternity with them were destined for limbo, but even limbo could not hold them forever. In the general resurrection of the dead they would rise as young adults, perfect in body and soul, to find the earth prepared to receive them. In the final agony of time the earth would be reborn, swept clean and bright by some celestial fire, made ready for its new role in eternity. The children of limbo had been deprived of their supernatural birthright by original sin, but this sin had not robbed them of their destiny as human beings. As citizens of the new earth, total victors over death, they would achieve the natural happiness that lies within the powers of man. Their knowledge of God through his creation would be far greater than that of any philosopher known to us. And they would grow wiser and more contented in this knowledge throughout all eternity.

Politi was not the first theologian to speak of unbaptized children spending their eternity in a renovated world. The Franciscan Nicola Lyrinense had suggested the idea half a century earlier. And even that gloomy monk of Florence, Savonarola, had mentioned it in his sermons.[2] Politi's contribution was to place the children of the new earth in a remarkable relation both to heaven and to Christ.

The Dominican theologian speaks first of the association that these young people will have with the angels and the saints. They are not exiles in the strict sense of the word, he observes, but rather those "who have been left behind." It seemed quite reasonable, then, that there should be a normal commerce between these sons of men and the adopted sons of God. According to Politi, the young men and women of the earthly paradise will find this companionship so profitable that nothing will be lacking to them aside from the beatific vision itself.

Remarkable as their association is with the blessed, however, it is overshadowed by their relation to Christ. If God's justice had been given full play, Politi remarks, these children would have borne God's displeasure forever in the subterranean gloom of limbo. The Redeemer interceded for them, however; and through his merits their sentence was commuted and they were admitted to the natural perfection that they had lost in Adam. The redemptive act of Christ was thus effectively extended not only to the adopted children of God but to these forgotten children of men. Christ united them both to himself, endowing the baptized with supernatural life, restoring natural perfection to those who were united to him by nature and who had not sinned in any way. Thus unbaptized children were freed from the law of death and put beyond the assaults of their ancient enemy, Satan.

Although Politi's ideas met with violent opposition in some quarters, they found a sympathetic hearing among theologians of the Society of Jesus. Salmeron, Molina, Lessius agreed that the children of limbo would enjoy a remarkable degree of happiness in the life to come, but it remained for the greatest Jesuit theologian of the century to bring the notion of limbo to its ultimate refinement.[3] This was Francisco Suarez.

FRANCISCO SUAREZ

Christ the Prince

In God's providence, said Suarez, a moment will come when Christ will be acknowledged by all men as Prince and Judge of the world. Since even unbaptized infants must pay him this homage, they will have their part to play both in the resurrection of the dead and in the final judgment of mankind.

They died as infants, but they will rise as adults possessing not only the use of their reason but full physical maturity as well. As young adults they will stand before the tribunal of Christ to see there for the first time the divine pattern into which their lives had been woven.

The Judgment

Children will all be present at the final judgment to see and honor the majesty of Christ, says Suarez, because the glory of Christ demands that he be adored and acknowledged by all as the Prince, the supreme Judge of the world. They could hardly pay proper tribute to Christ, however, if they were unaware of what was being done at this mighty tribunal. When they see the sentence of damnation passed upon the wicked as well as the joy of the just, they will recognize the justice of God. Their own destiny too, fixing them as it does on a middle ground between damnation and glory, will stand revealed as another manifestation of God's perfect justice.

Will they be aware of the fact that they all bear within them the stain of original sin? Suarez thinks that they will. First of all they pay homage to Christ the Redeemer of the human race; this they could hardly do without being aware of the implications of the redemption. They will know then why the just are saved, and they will know that the wicked have contemned the redemptive act of Christ. Their knowledge, however, will not be that of faith but of reason, gathered from what they see and hear.[4] The whole plan of providence will be opened to them; while acknowledging Christ as God, they will honor his Father for the great gift they received first in Adam and then in Christ.

Their Fate

Theologians like Soto and St. Bonaventure thought the children doomed to spend their eternity in some gloomy place, but Suarez thinks differently, because they have done nothing to merit a sentence of damnation, though they are unworthy of heaven. At the last judgment, he feels, hell will become such a place of horrors that limbo's proximity would borrow of its terror.[5]

Since children are guilty of no personal sin, the suffering that such a place would necessarily imply seems unfair and uncalled-for. It seems consonant with the pity of Christ that he would let them live out their eternity upon the earth, a congenial climate for the vigorous natural resources they possess.

What will this world be like? Suarez holds that it will be

totally made over after the resurrection of the dead. When the judgment has been completed the world will be swept away and the very air will burst into flames, consuming the earth, purging it of every impurity, leaving behind a new world gleaming in brilliant splendor. In this new universe the children of Adam will live out their eternal exile from the kingdom of God.[6]

Their Bodies

As we have already seen, Suarez suggests that their bodies will be those of adults, completely adapted to the full and perfect use of reason. God's providence will not only shield them from harm but eternally free them of any need for food or drink. The unremitting strife that man experiences from concupiscence will be unknown to them. Their passions will be perfectly subject to their will and their will to their reason. The disorderly contention of the lower appetites and the higher will find no place in the new world in which they live.[7]

Their Minds

This quiescence of their disorderly passions, says Suarez, will have its effect on their minds too. Unhampered by their passions, unimpeded by the distractions that bother men in this life, they will bring to perfection in themselves every natural virtue: justice, wisdom, courage, prudence. The natural law which the wounded children of Adam found beyond their strength in life will be well within the powers of the citizens of the new world. Beatitude too will be possible to them—the possession of God by their natural powers of intellection and volition. Unimpeded by either concupiscence or temptation, their minds will be able to contemplate God, their wills to love him above all things. In this, then, they attain not the supernatural end for which God destined them but the natural end for which their natures crave.[8]

Christ Their Prince and Leader

These children, Suarez says, will be present at the last judgment to pay homage to the God-Man for his redemptive work. Although they failed to share in the real fruits of his redemption—adoptive sonship and a heavenly heritage—they did profit from the redemptive work of Christ.

If God had desired to exercise the full rigor of his justice, says Suarez, he might have condemned these children to the flames of hell. They were, after all, children of wrath and vessels of anger because of original sin. If their destiny, instead of being an eternal horror, is an eternal paradise, then this must be attributed to the merits of Christ, who offered his Father satisfaction not only for every personal sin that man might commit but also for the original sin that stained every human nature that came into the world.[9]

SUAREZ AND A REACTION

The theories of Suarez were a high-water mark in the development of the limbo theology. His splendid vision was shortly to become an important element in a controversy that was to endure for the next two centuries. The Jesuit theologian had moved as far as possible from the views of Augustine without actually admitting unbaptized infants to the kingdom of God. His ideas were symptomatic of a rigorous new theology that was willing to reappraise the past and where necessary even to reshape it. A violent reaction to the new theology was taking shape, however; it involved a rediscovery of the past that revived and revitalized many of the ideas of Augustine, including his views on the fate of unbaptized infants. One of the most important elements in this reaction was the Protestant Reformation.

THE RETURN TO AUGUSTINE

The intellectual topography of Europe was profoundly altered by the Reformation. Not only did it tear loose a great segment of the body Catholic, it jettisoned some of the most important centuries of Catholic thought. The Reformers passed over the Middle Ages in their "Return to the Gospel" and buttressed their doctrine with the authority of Augustine. The Scholastics had not developed Augustine's thought, said the Protestants; they had betrayed it. By abandoning Augustine the Catholic Church had permitted Pelagianism to invade its theology. The only course that seemed open to the Reformers was to turn back to the saint himself, to recapture his views of grace and original sin. As we might suspect, this enthusiasm led to a revival of interest in the ancient opinion on the fate of unbaptized infants.[10]

The new direction Protestantism had taken awakened sympathetic echoes in the Catholic camp. A new reverence for Augustine had begun to spread through the Catholic universities of Europe; and men began to turn to his writings for inspiration in their wrestling with new problems. The anti-Pelagian works of Augustine were read and reread by the theologians of the day. Studded as they are with references to unbaptized infants, they began to exercise a growing influence;[11] and increasing numbers of Catholic theologians began to abandon the scholastic idea of limbo. The most prominent of these was Denis Petau, a French Jesuit.

Petau was something of a trail-blazer; he walked alone down a new path, opening the way to a theology that was less speculative and more thoroughly grounded in the literature of the patristic age. While this quiet scholar did not scorn speculation, he did believe in turning back history's pages to see what foundation there might be for it. In his own blunt way he said that Augustine's views of unbaptized children were not an appendage to this theology but an important part of it. Moreover, said Petau, it was an opinion that had been endorsed by many of the Fathers and probably sanctioned by the Council of Florence.[12] There would be many who followed him in his thoughtful analysis; some of them, however, lost their sense of perspective. Known to history as the Jansenists, they began a debate on the fate of unbaptized infants that lasted for 150 years and ultimately involved the Jesuits and the Augustinians.

THE LIMBO DEBATE: STAGE ONE, JANSENISTS VS. JESUITS

The origins of Jansenism are to be sought in the Protestant Reformation.[13] Catholic theologians who came to grips with the new Protestant theology were impressed by its contempt for Scholasticism and its devotion to Augustine. The theologians of Louvain were among the first into the fray with Protestantism, and perhaps they were most strongly influenced by it. Baius, the university's Chancellor, tried to defeat Protestantism with its own weapons; he cut himself badly. Twice censured by Rome, his theology lived on in Jacques Janson and Cornelius Jansenius, his successors at Louvain.

While Jansenism took its direction from the Reformation, it got its momentum from the Renaissance. Appalled by the skepticism of the Renaissance, the Jansenists called for a return to antiquity. They proposed to lead the Church away from scholastic error and back to the patristic conception of revelation. Their natural antagonists were the Jesuits, who hoped to Christianize the new Humanism instead of running from it. Rather than abandon the work of the Middle Ages, they had begun the tedious work of cutting away the tangled growth of centuries in order to reveal the splendor of Scholasticism. Two groups so diametrically opposed could not long avoid a collision; the clash occurred in 1640 with the publication of the *Augustinus,* the work of Cornelius Jansenius.

The *Augustinus* presented itself as a disinterested study of Augustine; in reality it was a defense of Baius. Baius had set up Augustine's treatises on grace as the sole source of orthodox Catholic teaching on the subject. Jansenius too believed that the neglect of Augustine lay at the root of the Church's troubles. His boundless admiration for Augustine led him into a vicious attack on Scholasticism and on the Jesuits who championed it.

The *Augustinus* was a raking broadside that swept across the theology of some of the most prominent Jesuits. Among the "Jesuit ideas" under attack was the notion of limbo. "Scholastics," said Jansenius, "who gave natural happiness or immunity from eternal fire to infants dying unbaptized had departed far from the mind of Augustine and perhaps of the Church, which had condemned the Pelagians according to his principles."[14]

The Jesuits at Louvain had been forewarned of the *Augustinus*. When they found they could not prevent its publication, they attacked it vigorously in a number of theses. These theses are important because they mark both the objections to Jansenius and the method of attack that the Jesuits employed during the next 150 years. Two of the points scored by the Jesuits are of particular interest. First they defended the scholastic idea of limbo; secondly they toned down the Jansenists' exaggerated reverence for Augustine. These two ideas thus gained a permanent place in the Jansenist-Jesuit debate; often they seem inseparable.[15]

By proclaiming himself the oracle of Augustine, Jansenius proved himself a master strategist. At a single stroke he gained prestige for his doctrine and laid a trap for his opponents. Augustine's authority was, of course, more than enough to gain a hearing for an idea in the seventeenth-century world of theology. It was also a rock on which an adversary might dash himself to pieces. Unfortunately many of Jansenius' adversaries fell into the trap. Two alternatives were open to them as they planned their assault on Jansenism. They could attack the doctrine as an exaggeration of Augustine; or they could turn on Augustine himself and try to minimize his importance. The second course was a perilous one when we recall the temper of the times. A strong Augustinian current was then running through the theological schools of France and Belgium. Any theologian who tried tampering with the prestige of Augustine found himself sailing a narrow channel between Scylla and Charybdis. Unusual discretion was necessary for one to question Augustine's authority without offending his votaries. Unfortunately polemics do not breed discretion, and a number of authors sailed into trouble. One of them was Richard Simon.

Bossuet and the Fate of Unbaptized Infants

Simon had little regard for the Fathers in general, but he felt a particular aversion for St. Augustine. His *Histoire Cri-*

tique is famous in the history of biblical criticism.[16] A *cause célèbre* in its own day, it found an implacable adversary in Jacques Bossuet, the Bishop of Meaux. Bossuet lists his grievances against Simon in an indignant crescendo. Simon had accused Augustine of breaking away from Christian tradition, formulating a whole new theory of grace, and authoring the ideas of Luther, Calvin, and Jansenius. The only thing to do was to abandon him to the Jansenists. Among the Augustinian ideas which Simon couldn't stomach was the one which would damn an unbaptized child to hell.

Bossuet's rebuttal was incisive and devastating; and in a sweeping defense he championed Augustine's ancient opinion on the fate of infants. According to Bossuet, both the Council of Lyons and the Council of Florence had said that original sin would be punished in hell. There could be only one conclusion, said Bossuet: the children are in hell, in perpetual torment.[17]

Bossuet's views are in keeping with his devotion to St. Augustine. He has been called the man "who most exactly reproduced the thought and manner of St. Augustine among the moderns."[18] Although Bossuet was not in the mainstream of the growing rejection of limbo, his ideas are important, for they show us how deeply the Augustinian revival had begun to penetrate the theological world.

THE LIMBO DEBATE: STAGE TWO, AUGUSTINIANS VS. JESUITS

Three Jesuit theologians figure more directly than Bossuet in the growing debate over limbo; their names were Adam, Annat, and Moraines. They are memorable for having occasioned the writing of one of the most explosive books of seventeenth-century theology—the *Vindiciae Augustinianae* of Henry Noris. Using the severity of Augustine's theology as a fulcrum, the Jesuits tried to tumble him from the pedestal on which the Jansenists had placed him. His anti-Pelagian writings, they said, distorted the truth and smacked of heresy. In another century the accusation would have been reckless; under the circumstances it was disastrous. For it drove a wedge between Catholic theologians at a moment when they should have been closing ranks. The Augustinians gave the first evidence of the split when they chose Henry Noris to defend the honor of Augustine and their order.[19]

Noris was an unusual man. Von Pastor ranks him with Mabillon as one of the most important scholars of the seventeenth century.[20] English by ancestry, Italian by birth, he became a member of the Hermits of St. Augustine. In the vanguard of the Augustinian revival, he formulated what has become known as the "Strict Augustinian School" of theological thought. During his lifetime he enjoyed the favor of several popes; and after his death Benedict XIV came to his defense with an extraordinary *apologia*. Noris wrote bitingly and well and with an immense amount of erudition. His object, he said, was to free Augustine from the calumnies that had been heaped on him by "recent writers."[21] He refrained from naming names for the most part, but the Jesuits were clearly under fire. If we would really understand Noris's position, however, we must see it not only as a reaction to the Jesuits but as an attempt to snatch Augustine back from the Jansenists. The one objective drove him close to the Jansenist camp; the other kept him within the pale of orthodoxy. It would not always be easy for his opponents to see this, however, and he was often denounced as a Jansenist.

His *Historia Pelagiana* set off an explosion that reverberated throughout Europe for seventy-five years. Jesuit theologians were indignant at an attack from this quarter while they fought the enemies of the Church; and they made heroic efforts to have Noris's book condemned. It was examined by the Holy See on three occasions and each time released without censure of any sort. As we shall see, this point will figure prominently in the debate between the Jesuits and the Augustinians.

Augustinians vs. Limbo

Noris was not a speculative theologian; following the lead of the Jesuit Petau, he combined a good theological training with an immense historical scholarship. Probing into the past, he found little historical justification for the limbo of the Scholastics. The Scholastics had placed unbaptized infants within the confines of hell; but they set them apart from the damned by denying that they suffered the pain of sense or any distress over the loss of heaven. In Noris's opinion the Scholastics were at variance with the pontiffs, the councils, the Fathers of the past. The punishment meted out to an unbaptized child was identical generically and specifically with that given one who died in the state of actual serious sin. The only difference between the two was one of degree. Original sin was the least of the serious sins; and hence it was punished least severely.

There would be no point in minimizing the boldness of Noris's thesis. He clearly denied the limbo of Thomas and Bonaventure, the "house of shadows" where children lived without sadness, free of pain. He vigorously rejected the idea of any natural happiness for these infants. He quite candidly assigned children to the punishment of the flames of hell, although he willingly conceded that their punishment was the mildest among the damned. He was bold, too, in saying that the Scholastics had erred through ignorance of the history of the Pelagian controversy. For all of his boldness, however, Noris didn't lose his sense of perspective. He conceded that these were his opinions and, he believed, Augustine's; he did not think them beyond question. His one purpose, he asserted, was to prove that Augustine had not distorted the truth in his anti-Pelagian zeal but that he had built a solidly probable case against an infant limbo in eternity.[22]

Noris's argument was built up with a fair amount of logic and, as we have noted, a great deal of erudition. He knew Augustine; and he knew the period in which Augustine had written. And he used every resource at his command to prove that Augustine's ideas were those of his age and not simply the aberrations of a man distracted during a heated controversy. His methods stand in sharp contrast to those of Jansenius. The author of the *Augustinus* staked his entire argument on the authority of Augustine; and with Augustine the argument stood or fell. Jansenius' objective was different too. He saw the Molinist conception of limbo as another proof that the Jesuits had abandoned Augustine for his Pelagian adversaries. Noris was not above sarcasm, but he made no accusations of heresy. The question of limbo had obvious polemical possibilities, however; and Noris exploited them. The Jesuits who occasioned his book had used Augustine's ideas on unbaptized children to minimize his authority, accusing him of going to extremes. Noris turned the tables and demanded to know what historical justification the Jesuits or the Scholastics could offer for the idea of limbo. It would seem, he concluded, that it was they who had gone to extremes.

The man who developed Noris's system and carried it well into the eighteenth century was John Laurent Berti, an Italian and an Augustinian. The General of the Augustinians, Sciaffinati, told Berti to write a book that would set forth the whole of Augustine's thought but especially his views of grace and free will. When it was completed, the book was to serve as a text for the students of the entire Augustinian Order. The result of Berti's labors was the massive *Opus de Theologicis Disciplinis*.[23] Its semi-official character helps to explain the prominence that the views of Noris and Berti achieved. Their opinions were not simply the private views of theologians; they were those of the Augustinian Order.

The Reformation had cost the Augustinians many of their three thousand monasteries, but they still remained a formidable factor in Catholic Europe. When the views of Noris and Berti were adopted by the Augustinians, the denial of limbo had penetrated very far indeed into the thinking of Catholic theologians. The semi-official character of Berti's work was one of his main lines of defense when he was denounced to the Holy Office as a Jansenist. His doctrine, said Berti, was that of the Augustinians, and especially of those who followed Noris.[24] The Augustinians agreed. When the Augustinian General, Vasquez, broke off scholastic relations with the Jesuits, he listed among his grievances the accusations which they had levelled against Berti and which, he said, reflected upon the entire Order.[25] This same "Augustinian" character of Berti's book does much to explain the pope's caution in dealing with the requested condemnation of Berti. He very much feared, he said, that such a condemnation would start a conflagration that would spread to the ends of the earth.[26]

There were now three major participants in the limbo debate; the Jansenists, the Jesuits, and the Augustinians. The Jansenists denied limbo and accused its Jesuit defenders of Pelagianism. In their rebuttal Jesuit theologians angered the Augustinians, who then came to the defense of their patron. In the discussion that followed there were times when it was difficult for some of the Jesuit theologians to distinguish Jansenist from Augustinian, and heated accusations were often made. Indeed there was more fire than light in the discussion as it moved from the seventeenth into the eighteenth century. Accusations and denunciations were frequent; and none were more irresponsible than those made by the Jansenists, especially the Italian Jansenists. Up till recent times the history of Italian Jansenism has been little known; yet Jansenism and the limbo debate reached its culmination in Italy in the person of Pietro Tamburini.

THE LIMBO DEBATE: STAGE THREE, ITALIAN JANSENISTS VS. LIMBO

Born in 1734 in Brescia, Tamburini was educated for the priesthood through the generosity of several priests who recognized his unusual talents. Assigned to teach philosophy and theology in the seminary at Brescia, Tamburini published his *Summa de Gratia* in 1771,[27] decrying the evils that flowed from the teachings of the famous Jesuit Molina. His theme was traditional among the Jansenists, the need of returning to Sacred Scripture and tradition. The founts of revelation, he said, found their correct interpretation in the theology of the Augustinians, not in the "twisted syllogisms" of those who rationalized divine truth. The book created a furor, and Tamburini was relieved of his seminary position. For a while he acted as prefect of studies at the Irish College at Rome, but once again complaints were made of his Jansenistic proclivities, and he was forced to leave the Holy City. It was a major step in his career. The Austrian rulers were trying to convert into so many rights the privileges that had been given them by the popes. To defend these "rights" Prince Kaunitz was looking for theologians to fill the professorial chairs of Vienna and Pavia. Tamburini proved himself one of the ablest of them. The emperor showed his appreciation by making him Rettore Magnifico of the University of Pavia.[28]

During these years Tamburini's position was a prominent one, for Pavia gained renown as one of the foremost centers of learning in Italy; and during the Emperor Joseph's reign, it held the attention of Europe. Its rector rapidly gained a reputation as a *caposcuola* (cultural leader), and as such he gave tone and direction to the Jansenist movement in Italy.

In the question of unbaptized children Tamburini carried on where Jansenius had left off. The *Augustinus* had insinuated that Augustine's views were a dogma of faith; Tamburini openly proclaimed it to be a fact. He went a good deal farther than Jansenius had gone. He used what he termed the Pelagian fable of limbo to hew away at Jesuit theologians as well as to defend his own brand of Jansenism.

As we mentioned, Tamburini's *Summa de Gratia* was the opening salvo in his war against the Jesuits. Carrying on in true Jansenist tradition, Tamburini developed at length the alleged parallel between the Jesuits and the Pelagians. The Jesuit Molina, said Tamburini, had quite obviously drawn certain opinions from Pelagian sources; his views on the fate of infants clearly illustrated this Pelagian character of his plagiarism.[29] This one Jesuit error, however, was symptomatic of a far more serious fallacy, their erroneous conception of original sin.[30] The Jesuits, of course, made no attempt to deny original sin; the matter had been too obviously decided by the Church. Nevertheless, said Tamburini, they had managed to eviscerate the doctrine, leaving nothing more than the name. Original sin, they would say, consists of nothing more than the privation of sanctifying grace; it could not, therefore, be a sin in the true sense of the word. Was it any wonder, asked Tamburini, that they had championed the idea of limbo? Having denied that original sin was truly a sin, they logically had to deny that there was any punishment for it. Consequently they placed unbaptized children in a middle place where there was neither suffering nor glory but a "sort of happiness." This was the clear teaching not only of Molina but of his confreres: Salmeron, Vasquez, Suarez, and Becanus.[31]

Limbo was useful to Tamburini not only as a handy weapon against the Jesuits but as a defense for his own theological system. To understand this tactic we should recall the circumstances in which he wrote. Jansenism was dying in France; it was restricted to a small circle of intellectuals in Italy. In spite of his powerful patrons Tamburini must have felt like a man against the world. Casting about for a way to give prestige to his ideas, he hit on a notion that seemed to promise the help he needed. According to this theory the Jansenists were the one small group who clung to the ancient truths of Christendom and in whom Christ's promise of indefectibility was fulfilled. Christ had promised his Church that she would always possess the truth, said Tamburini; he had not assured her that a majority of her faithful would always believe it. It was possible, then, that a dogma once believed by all could fall into obscurity, forgotten by all but a handful in whom Christ's promise was fulfilled.

Tamburini found the tessera of truth in antiquity. The closer a doctrine's link to apostolic times, the purer and more certain it became. If this link were broken, if at some time a doctrine had not been taught, or the contrary had been taught, then it was clear that the doctrine was not of apostolic origin. A good example of this, said Tamburini, was the limbo fable. It was

already some five or six centuries old; but in apostolic times
the contrary had been taught. This was certain because Augustine himself had attacked the fable, drawing his teaching
from the apostles. The age of the limbo fable and the con-
spiracy of the Schools in defending it only served to show, said
Tamburini, that a revealed doctrine could exist in the Church
in almost complete obscurity.[32] In this ingenious use of the
idea of limbo, Tamburini found the strength that numbers
failed to give him. His Jansenist band was the brave little group
clinging to apostolic truth in an age that had forgotten it.

Tamburini's ideas might have died with him, but instead
they achieved immortality of a sort in the Jansenist Synod of
Pistoia. The synod opened on September 18, 1786, after
months of planning by Bishop Ricci and Peter Leopold, the
Archduke of Tuscany and brother of the Austrian emperor.
Ricci and Leopold hoped that the synod would be the first
step toward an independent Church of Tuscany. As a result
Pistoia's importance goes beyond anything warranted by an
ordinary gathering of simple priests. The plans of its promoters
gave it a national character, while the presence of Tamburini
made it the official expression of Italian Jansenism.

Tamburini fully exploited the despotic control which, thanks
to Ricci, he held over synodal procedure. So many of the
synod's "decisions" were taken verbatim from Tamburini's
books that it is obvious he came to Pistoia with the decrees
already prepared and in his brief case.[33] The "Fathers of the
synod" approved them with a minimum of discussion, duti-
fully adopting the Jansenist view of grace and predestination;
as a corollary, they rejected the "Pelagian fable of limbo" and
consigned unbaptized infants to the torments of hell in company with Satan and his angels.[34]

The synod closed September 28th to the complete satisfaction of Leopold, who ratified its resolutions within a week. The archduke's endorsement proved Pistoia's undoing. Spurred into action, Pius VI began the investigation that terminated in the Bull *Auctorem Fidei,* a deathblow to Jansenism and a milestone in the history of limbo.

THE CHURCH AND THE LIMBO CONTROVERSY

In the three centuries that followed the council of Trent the limbo controversy constantly simmered and sometimes boiled over. Augustinians and Jansenists denied the existence of limbo; Jesuits defended it. The Jansenists detested the Jesuits, the Jesuits reciprocated, and the Augustinians disliked them both. The air was charged with suspicion and at times with libel. The Jesuits were denounced as Pelagians; the Augustinians as Jansenists; and the Jansenists, rightly enough, as heretics. As the Spanish historian La Fuente remarked:

> "Theology was a chaos of subtleties disputed with such acrimony and exasperation that the different schools professed a hatred for one another that they might well have had for the heretics."[35]

The controversy became so heated that denunciations and counter-appeals were made to the Holy See. The circumstance was a happy one for later theologians for the light it cast on the question of unbaptized infants. In the course of the three centuries that followed the Protestant Reformation the Church passed judgment repeatedly on the limbo theories of the Jansenists and the Augustinians as they were brought before her. Since her reaction to each was strikingly different, we will consider the cases separately.

THE AUGUSTINIANS AND THE CHURCH

In Italy feeling ran high against the Protestants in the year immediately following Luther's break with the Church. As frequently happens in such circumstances, Catholics saw Protestants lurking behind every tree. An Augustinian preacher, Augustine Mainardi, was denounced to Rome for preaching erroneous, un-Catholic doctrines; among his ideas was a denial of limbo. Children who die with original sin on their souls, he said, are damned to the eternal torment of the fires of hell. Luther himself had denied any middle ground between heaven and hell to unbaptized children; and when Mainardi championed the same view, he was denounced as un-Catholic. The monk appealed his case to Pope Paul III, submitting a list of his ideas and asking that the Pope himself judge whether or not they were Catholic in tone. When Paul's advisers pronounced Mainardi's teaching "Catholic and not erroneous," the pope allowed him to continue his preaching. Mainardi's view of unbaptized infants, said Paul, was that of St. Augustine himself, and could be found in many of the saint's writings.[36] The pope repeated his observation three years later when another Augustinian, Musaeus of Trivigiano, was denounced for denying the existence of limbo.[37]

Henry Noris and the Holy Office

A century passed before the question was again submitted to Rome; by this time the Jansenist controversy was blowing full gale, and the man accused was Henry Noris. Noris, who emphatically denied the existence of limbo in his *Historia Pelagiana,* saw the book reviewed by the Holy Office on three distinct occasions: 1672, 1676, and 1692. Each time the decision of the Congregation was favorable; and after each examination

Noris was rewarded in some way by the Holy See. In 1673 he was appointed to the Inquisition itself; in 1676 he was given a promotion within the Holy Office; and in 1695 he was made a cardinal member of the Inquisition with the titular church of St. Augustine. The irony of these appointments could not have been entirely lost on his accusers.[38]

Strangely enough, opposition to Noris re-formed after his death for one final attack. In 1757 his book was placed on the Index of the Spanish Inquisition. When Benedict XIV protested, the Spanish king ordered an investigation. His Inquisitor General reported that the new edition of the Spanish Index had been prepared by two Jesuits, Casani and Guerrero. These two men, he said, took it upon themselves to place Noris's books on the Index without informing the Inquisitor General and without any preliminary examination.

In a letter to the Spanish Inquisitor, Perez de Prado, Benedict demanded that Noris's books be removed from the Index.[39] The Holy See, said the Pope, had repeatedly investigated the works of Noris, and nothing had been found deserving condemnation or any other censure. Convinced of the soundness of Noris's doctrine, Benedict continued, Pope Innocent had first appointed him consultor and then cardinal of the Holy Office. In view of these facts the Spanish Inquisition had no business examining Noris's works, much less condemning them.

At this moment one of those unfortunate incidents occurred that embarrass heads of state. The pope, who had confined his protests to diplomatic channels, showed a copy of his letter to the Augustinians. The triumphant Augustinians published the letter, and the consequent publicity embarrassed and enraged the Spanish Inquisition. Spain vigorously protested that so delicate a matter should have been kept secret. Spanish pride was now as much an issue as Noris himself, and years passed before Benedict could force the removal of Noris's name from Spain's Index of forbidden books.[40]

Giovanni Berti

In the meanwhile another Augustinian was receiving unwelcome attention from the Inquisition. Giovanni Berti, like Noris before him, denied the existence of limbo; and like Noris he was vigorously denounced to Rome. This time the accusers were two French bishops, de Saleons of Vienne and Languet of Sens. Benedict XIV replied to de Saleons that Berti's book had been submitted to competent theologians; and although they disagreed with Berti's opinions they judged them nevertheless to be sound.[41]

In a letter to the bishop of Sens, the pope said that nothing had been found in Berti's writings that was contrary to the decisions of the Church.[42]

Clement XIII and the Augustinian Manifesto

In 1758 Rome was called on to re-evaluate the appraisal it had made of the Augustinians over the preceding two centuries. The struggle with the Jansenists was approaching its climax. In an atmosphere clouded by controversy it was no mean task to distinguish an Augustinian from a Jansenist, and more than one theologian failed to do so. The Augustinians found themselves denounced as Jansenist and their theology pilloried as heterodox. At this juncture the Augustinian General, Vasquez, appealed to Rome, claiming that the Jesuit theologians of France, Spain, and Italy had accused his men of heresy. He submitted a formal petition to Clement XIII, asking that the Augustinian School be protected against the calumnies of its enemies.

Vasquez' petition contained what might be termed a manifesto of Augustinian theology, embracing twenty-three propositions fundamental to Augustinian teaching; among them was a denial of limbo:

> "Unbaptized children who die in original sin are not only distressed by the loss of the Beatific Vision, but they are tormented by the pain of fire in hell, however mildly it may be. [This opinion] is in keeping with the opinions of St. Augustine."[43]

Clement submitted the matter to the cardinals of the Holy Office; and on January 10, 1759, a decree was drawn up and approved by him. The decree itself contained nothing new. It simply referred to the decisions of Paul III and to the action taken by Rome in the cases of Noris and Berti. With these previous decisions, Clement said, the security of the Augustinian School has been sufficiently provided for; it need have no fears.[44] Since we have already seen the decisions to which Clement refers, we can now evaluate the status of the Augustinian denial of limbo at the close of the eighteenth century.

The Augustinians taught that an unbaptized infant must suffer the fires of hell, however mild these might be. The papal decrees did not, except in the broadest sense of the word, approve the Augustinian theory; but neither did they disapprove of it. While theologians were free to disagree with the Augustinians, they could not censure the Augustinian position without disapproving what Rome had not disapproved in the persons of Paul III, Benedict XIV, and the popes who had caused Noris's writings to be so thoroughly reviewed.[45]

THE JANSENISTS AND THE CHURCH

Noris and Berti denied limbo; their books were reviewed and "approved" by Rome. Tamburini denied Limbo; and his writings were condemned by the Roman Inquisition almost without exception. We know too that his denial of limbo was incorporated into the Jansenist Synod of Pistoia, and in turn the synod was condemned by the famous bull of Pope Pius VI, *Auctorem Fidei,* in 1794.

Some theologians think that Pius here revoked the earlier "approval" the papacy had given the Augustinians and established limbo once and for all as Catholic doctrine. Others feel that *Auctorem Fidei* did nothing at all to enhance the theological value of the idea of limbo. Before commenting on these opinions, it would be well to recall what it was that Tamburini taught and what part of his doctrine had been adopted by the Synod of Pistoia.

Tamburini declared that Augustine's view of unbaptized infants was a dogma of the Catholic faith; it was a doctrine proclaimed by the Fathers and accepted by the councils of the Church. Engrossed in logical gymnastics and oblivious of Church history, the medieval theologians abandoned this dogma; and it entered on a period of obscurity. The Church herself ceased to insist upon it and instead tolerated the limbo theory which was now favored by so many theologians. Augustine's teaching, said Tamburini, ceased to be a doctrine of the Church because the Church ceased teaching it. For this reason the limbo thesis could not be denounced as heretical. Nevertheless it was untenable in view of the obvious teaching of the Fathers, the councils, and the Scriptures.

This was the thesis of Tamburini, and this was the stand taken by the Synod of Pistoia in 1784. The synod deplored the obscurity into which the most important truths of the faith had fallen; and it rejected limbo as a Pelagian fable, insisting that unbaptized children will suffer the torment of fire.

There are two distinct ideas enmeshed in the Jansenist denial of limbo. In common with the Augustinians and many other Catholic theologians they denied limbo, teaching that unbaptized children will suffer the pain of sense. Secondly they libelled their opponents by labelling limbo a "Pelagian fable." In drafting a condemnation of Pistoia, Pius VI took note of these two ideas and condemned one and not the other.

Overruling the protests of the Archduke Leopold, Pius VI directed Cardinal Gerdil to prepare a condemnation of the Synod of Pistoia.[46] The cardinal did his work meticulously, using a method that allowed the greatest precision. In each of its eighty-five articles *Auctorem Fidei* follows the same pattern. After listing a Jansenist proposition, it explains why the idea is objectionable and, in a final phrase, gives the Church's exact evaluation of the error.

After rejecting the Jansenist idea that a dogma of the faith could slip from the memory of the Church, Pius VI reviewed the Jansenist denial of limbo. Following Gerdil's carefully devised plan, he condemned the "doctrine" *which rejected limbo as a Pelagian fable.*[47] The entire weight of Pius' condemnation, therefore, fell not on the Jansenist denial of limbo but on the manner of the denial. The pope, therefore, did not reprimand the Jansenists for their denial of limbo but for the manner of their denial. According to the Synod of Pistoia, limbo was part and parcel of the Pelagian heresy; and this, said Pius, was false as well as insulting to a great number of Catholic theologians.

If Pius did nothing to enhance the dogmatic value of limbo, he did pull a troublesome thorn from the side of the Jesuits.

As we saw, limbo theology reached its ultimate development in Suarez and a few of his Jesuit colleagues, who would not only free children from any possible suffering in the world to come but would also assign them a remarkable degree of happiness. When the Jansenists accused Suarez and his confreres of a return to Pelagianism, Pius VI came to their rescue. The pope pointed out that the Pelagians had been condemned for teaching the existence of a middle ground characterized by neither guilt nor punishment. This observation was enough to vindicate the Jesuits' view of limbo. The concepts of Suarez and his fellow theologians gave infants a great deal of natural happiness, but they never forgot that limbo was not a state of innocence. The children would remain eternally guilty of original sin because for all eternity they would lack the grace that God had planned for them. Even in the final development of the doctrine, therefore, limbo bore only a superficial resemblance to the paradise of the Pelagian heresy.

FREEDOM OF THEOLOGIANS

During the centuries of the limbo controversy the Church refrained from taking sides. She stepped into the dispute repeatedly, but only to lay down certain rules. Limbo might be defended; it might be rejected; the Church made it clear that neither the defenders nor the opponents of limbo had the right to censure their antagonists. The Church's action may seem indefinite, but actually it brought an end to the long dispute. By insisting on the orthodoxy of both Augustinians and limbo theologians the Holy See robbed the question of much of its forensic value. Limbo is a highly speculative problem; it arouses interest and tempers when it is tied to a more volatile issue. This was true in the fourth and fifth centuries when it was linked to the denial of original sin. It was true in the seventeenth and eighteenth centuries when it was brought into the Jansenist controversy. Jansenius first propelled the question into prominence with his attack on the Jesuit theologians. Charges of "Jansenist" and "Pelagian" kept the issue alive. The papal decisions of 1758 and 1794 drew the sting from the controversy, and the dispute itself did not long survive. The Church treated the doctrine of limbo and the denial of limbo simply as "opinions" of theologians; she has been content with her decision to the present day.

During the nineteenth century the limbo question retreated to the comparative obscurity of a theological scholion. For all practical purposes the controversy was dead; nevertheless, it left its mark on theological thought. Although the great majority of theologians in the period returned to the scholastic notion of limbo, they were not sure where the idea stood in its relation to revelation. "A common opinion, a debated question" were the descriptions most often used by the theologians. Nor has the picture changed drastically in the twentieth century. While there was for a while a tendency to give greater theological weight to the notion of limbo, the majority of theologians have seen it as no more than a theological opinion. In very recent years a growing literature has been calling for a re-evaluation of the entire question.

To my surprise I discovered that the idea of limbo apparently failed to take root very deeply in the minds of the faithful during the nineteenth or twentieth centuries. Using the catechetical literature of the period as a measuring device, we find that in the nineteenth century only half the catechists surveyed taught the existence of limbo; and only two of these mentioned it by name. Of the twentieth-century catechetical writings, one-third of the sixty-six tabulated could be said to teach the doctrine of limbo, while only one author in six mentioned it by name.

In view of its tortured history—the decisions of the magisterium, the varied opinions of theologians, the lack of a clear persuasion among the faithful—we can only describe the doctrine of limbo as a theological opinion, a safe and rather widely accepted solution to a difficult problem.

Because it is an idea compounded of two distinct elements any investigation of limbo can revolve about either of its components and with quite different results. During the centuries of the limbo debate theologians asked whether unbaptized infants necessarily suffered the pains of hell in their exile from heaven. Another and quite distinct line of inquiry now asks whether such children are necessarily excluded from heaven. With this question we approach the extremely difficult problem of the salvation of an unbaptized child.

PART TWO

Modern Salvation Theories

IV

The Last Thirty Years

ALTERNATIVES TO THE IDEA OF LIMBO

The Augustinians rejected the doctrine of limbo because it seemed too radical a departure from Augustine and his contemporaries in the early Church. Another group of theologians who stand at quite the opposite end of the spectrum would admit unbaptized children to heaven. Limbo, they say, is incompatible with the salvific will of God. Their reasoning is not hard to follow. Adam had scarcely sinned before God promised him a redeemer, when he said to the Devil:

> "I will put enmity between you and the woman, between your seed and her seed; he shall crush your head and you shall lie in wait for his heel." (Gen. 3:15)

Here we have the first manifestation of God's desire to undo what man had done, to rebuild what man had destroyed. It is the first scriptural evidence that we possess of what men would come to call God's salvific will. God's sincere desire to save every human being, at first hinted at by sacred writers, was clarioned by St. Paul:

"This is good and agreeable in the sight of God our
Saviour, *who wishes all men to be saved* and to come
to the knowledge of the truth." (1 Tim. 2:4)

Obviously the existence of hell does nothing to diminish the
sincerity of God's salvific will. For a desire is not a command.
Should we choose to separate ourselves from God, he will
respect our choice and permit its consequences. In the case of
a child, however, the question of God's sincerity assumes an
added dimension. The child in limbo is separated from God
eternally, but through no choice of his own. Perhaps he died
before his Christian parents could baptize him. Perhaps his parents had never heard of baptism. Perhaps they knew of the
sacrament but neglected it. Death finds an unbaptized child
powerless to help himself and perhaps beyond the reach of help
from others. Can we say that God sincerely wills his salvation?
Theologians are hard pressed at this point to explain the salvific
will of God without explaining it away. Some of them have
given the whole business up as an impossible task. Rather than
attempt a reconciliation of the concepts of limbo and God's
salvific will, they suggest that we admit the incompatibility of
the two ideas and look elsewhere for a solution. Since limbo,
they say, rules out the sincerity of God's salvific will, limbo is
theologically unacceptable.

These theologians would insist that the children somehow or
other are saved, and thus eliminate what they see as a serious
objection against the sincerity of God's salvific will. Having
lopped off one of the hydra's heads, however, they find two
in its place. They must not only explain how these children
find their way into the kingdom of God, but they must reconcile their theory with the Church's teaching on the necessity
of baptism.

SOME ANCIENT SALVATION THEORIES

Salvation theories have been in existence in the Church for seventeen hundred years. Some of them have been condemned; not one of them has been has been encouraged. The oldest of them is probably that of Gregory of Nyssa. Gregory, as we recall, would not admit children to the kingdom of heaven "at once" because they were incapable of living the life of the blessed. Nonetheless he made some provision for their eventual entry into glory. He seemed to think that their embryonic faculties would develop through contemplation till at last they were capable of leading the life of heaven. This curious idea of Gregory's, we noted, seems to echo a much older theory of Origen, the *Apokatastasis*. Origen declared, of course, for the ultimate restoration of every living creature, angelic or human, infant or adult to union with God.

Augustine informs us that Vincentius Victor elaborated a theory somewhat like Gregory's and far more liberal than that proposed by the Pelagians. The Pelagians usually were content to impound unbaptized children in a sort of paradise between heaven and hell. Vincent, however, suggested that their exile in paradise would not be eternal. At the resurrection of the dead, he said, the infants will be admitted to heaven. Unfortunately, we know nothing more of Vincentius Victor. Our sole informant is Augustine; and he minces no words in his criticism of the hapless Vincent.[1]

Origen's restoration theories had a marked influence on many of the Greek theologians; and to this extent at least the salvation theories survived for a time in the East. They failed to win a general hearing either in the East or the West, however. And Origen's idea of "universal restoration" has long since been condemned by the Church.

The theologians of the Middle Ages, some of them at least, were able to concede a very limited exception to the law of baptism. Thomas and Bonaventure readily admitted that God's power was not restricted to his sacraments. As John was sanctified in the womb of Elizabeth, so by privileged exception God might give the grace of justification to whom he willed. Alexander of Hales agreed.[2]

Scholastic theologians conceded another exception to the law of baptism. William of Auxerre considered the case of a priest who would omit part of the form of a sacrament; through some inadvertence, let us say, he would fail to baptize in the name of the Father but only of the Son and the Holy Ghost. Since the form is not that decreed by our Lord, the sacrament would fail to produce an effect. William suggests, however, that in such a case, God himself would intervene to produce the effect of the sacrament.[3] Durandus extended this intervention to the case of a person who lacked the proper intention in administering a sacrament. In such a case, he said, Christ the High Priest would himself supply the intention.[4] We find a similar idea in St. Thomas Aquinas. We may believe, said Thomas, that Christ would intervene in the case of an unbaptized priest. Let us suppose a man had not been baptized, or perhaps he had been invalidly baptized, and in later life was ordained a priest. Since he lacks baptism, his ordination is invalid, and he possesses no priestly powers. Lest such a man spend his life administering the sacraments to no purpose, Thomas felt that Christ would supply the ultimate effect of these sacraments.[5] Since Thomas' ideas here are closely akin to those of Gregory and Durandus, there seems no reason why he would not have admitted their conclusions about the baptism of an infant.

Few theologians would quarrel with the suggestions of Bonaventure, Thomas and their confreres. Since the power of God is obviously not limited to the sacraments, there is the possibility that he would intervene directly to save a child dying without baptism. Since he is bound neither by the laws of grace nor of nature, he can step outside them whenever he chooses. The fact remains, however, that there are laws of both grace and nature, and these are the normal framework of his action. In the third chapter of St. John's Gospel we find Christ promulgating the law of baptism: ". . . unless a man be born again of water and the Spirit, he cannot enter the kingdom of God" (John 3:5). Because the medieval theologians acknowledged baptism as the law of salvation, they spoke of privileged exceptions. Had they gone further and made God's extra-sacramental intervention a normal thing, they would have postulated another law of salvation quite apart from the first. Lacking proof for the existence of such a law, they preferred to speak of exceptions to the law of baptism. And the exceptions to the laws of grace are as rare as exceptions to the laws of nature.

MORE MODERN THEORIES

The past few centuries have seen such a bewildering succession of salvation theories that any attempt to categorize them runs the risk of oversimplification. We may safely say, however, that with few exceptions they have the same respect for the law of baptism that characterized the medieval theologians. Some, it is true, would reappraise the law itself to determine whether it has *de facto* been universally promulgated. (Santos.)[6] Most, however, are content to admit the fact and to structure their theories about some form of baptism of desire. These we may divide into two categories, using the instant of death as a line of demarcation between them. For some the instant of death is important either because it is a moment of grace in which a choice is made or because it is itself a *votum reale* (real desire) of baptism. (Webb, Glorieux, Sauras.)[7] For others death itself plays no important role in the salvation of a child. They speak rather of a desire for baptism on the part of the child's parents, the Church, or the child itself in whom an objective transformation of some sort would constitute a *votum reale* of baptism. (Cajetan, Heris, Boudes, Mulders.)[8] Finally, there is a minority group who go beyond death in their search for a way to salvation. (Laurenge, Wilkin.)[9]

These are the hypotheses which form the substance of our fourth chapter. Others might have been included. But those we have chosen to describe seem representative of the "salvation" literature. Since they have all met varying degrees of opposition in the theological world, any balanced presentation of their ideas would be incomplete without a word or two of the criticism they have encountered.[10]

SANTOS: THE PROMULGATION OF THE GOSPEL

In his misseological study of the non-Christian world Angel Santos proposes a theory of salvation for the children of pagan parents, basing his suggestions on the possibility that the law of the gospel—and hence the law of baptism—has not been sufficiently proclaimed in every corner of the earth. From this premise he concludes that the primitive sacrament of nature retains its validity among these people to the present day.

The "sacrament of nature" is the term theologians have given to the primitive ritual which they feel must have existed among pre-Christian people to save their dying infants. An early description of it can be found in the *Summa Theologica* of St. Thomas Aquinas. "It is probable," Thomas said, "that parents directed to God some prayers and imparted a benediction to their children above all in danger of death. Those prayers and blessings were a sort of testimony of their faith."[11] Through this protestation of faith, theologians feel, the child was justified and found his way to heaven. This "sacrament of nature" was in keeping with the general plans of providence, for it placed responsibility for a child's salvation with his elders. The salvific will of God seemed to demand the existence of some such device if pre-Christian children were to have any chance for salvation. This primitive ritual was certainly superseded by circumcision for Jewish males, and is usually conceded to have been abrogated by the promulgation of the law of baptism. Santos, however, feels that "the sacrament of nature" may continue to exist where the gospel has not been adequately promulgated.

The principle that underlies his reasoning is readily admissible: where a law has not been promulgated it does not oblige. The problem therefore resolves itself into a question of fact: Has the gospel been sufficiently proclaimed everywhere? Or are there regions and peoples today among whom its precepts are not binding? Ancient theologians believed that the gospel had been adequately proclaimed in Palestine ten years after the death of Christ, and forty years later in the whole of the Roman Empire—an opinion that has long been abandoned.

Santos groups into three categories answers that have been given to the problem over the centuries:

1. Medieval theologians believed that the gospel had been sufficiently proclaimed everywhere and to everyone. Their optimistic views were certainly due to their fragmentary knowledge of the world in which they lived;

discoveries in the New World, Oceania, and the Far East put their theory completely out of date.

2. Suarez and most modern authors admit the possibility that there exist even today regions and individuals for whom the gospel has not been sufficiently proclaimed. This, however, is an accidental circumstance which does not affect the obligatory character of baptism, nor does it allow the sacrament of nature to retain its validity.[12]

3. Finally there is the opinion of Perrone, a nineteenth-century theologian. He argues from the principle that a divine positive law obliges only those to whom it is known. On this score, those to whom the gospel has not been sufficiently proclaimed are in the same state as the people who lived on earth before the coming of Christ.[13]

They could, therefore, employ the sacrament of nature to save their children. Santos' theory, of course, considers the objection which is drawn from a decree of the Council of Trent. Speaking of justification, the council defined it as a transferal to a state of grace and adoptive sonship which "after the promulgation of the gospel" could only be effected by baptism of water or baptism of desire. This phrase has been interpreted quite often to mean that the law of baptism has been in effect since the time of Christ. Santos' analysis of the Conciliar Acts leads him rather to conclude that Trent's only purpose was to define baptism as the method of regeneration proper to the New Testament. The council had no intention of taking a definite stand on the question of the precise moment or the extent of the gospel's promulgation.[14]

In adopting Perrone's theory, Santos does not say that all the infants of the non-Christian world are saved. He maintains only that the means still exist to save them—a proposition that rests on a number of observations. In the Gospels of

Matthew and Mark, for instance, the obligation of receiving baptism folllows on the proclamation of the gospel:

> "Go, therefore, and *make disciples* of all nations, *baptizing* them in the name of the Father, and of the Son, and of the Holy Spirit. . . ." (Matt. 28:19-20). "Go into the world and *preach* the gospel to every creature. He who believes and is *baptized* shall be saved." (Mark 16:15-16)

If Perrone's theory is not valid, Santos continues, then the coming of Christ would be enormously prejudicial to the salvation of these infants. Before his coming the means of their salvation was at hand. After his coming the sacrament of nature was rendered invalid by the law of baptism, and countless souls were left without a means of salvation.

Finally Santos argues that a rejection of Perrone's thesis would render unintelligible the Pauline comparison between Christ and Adam: "where the offense has abounded, grace has abounded yet more" (Rom. 5:20). In his well-known parallel between Christ and Adam Paul says that we are "sinners" because of Adam and "just" because of Christ. Christ redeemed us from sin and restored what we had lost in Adam. Yet if the law of baptism is in force everywhere on earth, then countless children are lost because of Adam and untouched by the grace of Christ. What meaning, then, could we reasonably give to those words of Paul: "grace has abounded yet more"?

Perrone's thesis has been severely criticized by Eduard Hugon,[15] who feels that it is at odds with the very clear teaching of Catholic tradition. No one, he says, has the right to introduce exceptions and dispensations when the language of the councils and the Fathers is so absolute. St. Augustine was certainly aware of vast regions where the gospel was unknown when he insisted on the absolute necessity of baptism. Nor did the Councils of Milevus, Florence, and Trent forget that there were idolatrous nations when they proclaimed without qualification the absolute necessity of the sacrament. But it is especially in the Council of Florence that every exception is excluded: "Make haste to baptize infants," for "there is no other remedy by which they can be helped other than the Sacrament of Baptism."

Moreover, it would have to be proved, says Hugon, that the sacrament of nature has a supernatural validity among pagan peoples today. We would have to be prepared to admit, he argues, that justification is possible without faith on the part of the one who is justified, on the part of his parents, or even the society in which they lived. Baptism, to be sure, gives grace even when the parents or the minister are without faith. But this grace is given in the name of the believing Church. In pre-Christian times those who made use of the sacrament of nature might lack this faith, but their society did not, and the rites they used were an external protestation of this faith. An admission of Perrone's thesis would compel us to say, therefore, that either the pagan society in question would have this faith or that justification was possible without faith. And who would be willing to take this position?

CARDINAL CAJETAN: BAPTISM OF DESIRE—
THE DESIRE OF THE PARENTS

Psychiatrists have uncovered a startling world of attraction and aversion in the infant mind, but they would be reluctant to describe it as a truly intellectual process. The possibility, therefore, of an infant conceiving and acting on a desire for God would seem to be too remote for serious consideration. Confronted by this human phenomenon, Cardinal Cajetan suggested that the desire for baptism is elicited not by the child but by its parents. His theory was inspired by a consideration of the sacrament of nature.

In the centuries before Christ, parents, as we have seen, could sanctify their children by some simple rite of consecration springing from their faith in God. This primitive ritual, known as the sacrament of nature, was superseded among the Chosen People by the "quasi-sacrament" of circumcision, but it remained in effect for the rest of mankind. At the heart of the sacrament of nature was the faith of the parents, expressing itself in the ways that nature and conscience suggested.

Struck by the implications of this primitive "sacrament," Cajetan suggested that the Christian parents of his own time might save their children by just such a consecration, should baptism prove impossible. A mother might sanctify a child dying in her womb, he said, if she blessed the baby, offered it to God, and invoked the Trinity. The child would thus be saved by baptism of desire although the desire was that of the parents and not that of the child. Cajetan argued that the faith of a Christian parent should be no less able to save a child than the faith of parents who lived and died before the coming of Christ. If the parents of pre-Christian times, he said, could justify their children by an act of faith and oblation, the men and women of the New Testament should be able to do as much.

We should note that at best Cajetan's theory offers only a partial solution to the problem of unbaptized children. It opens a way to heaven only for the children of responsible Christian parents, those who care enough for their faith and their children to look to their eternal salvation. The children of indifferent Christians or of non-Christian parents must look elsewhere for help. Admittedly, therefore, the cardinal's suggestion has its limitations. To hear his critics we would conclude that its shortcomings were radical indeed.

Cajetan argued that salvation should be a more facile matter in the Christian dispensation than it was in pre-Christian times; and therefore a means of salvation should be provided for every unbaptized infant. While his critics readily concede his principle, they will not admit that it guarantees his theory. It seems obvious to them that salvation is more readily accessible in the New Testament than it was in the Old. Baptism, they point out, is simpler and infinitely more certain than the "quasi-sacraments" of the time before Christ, since it demands nothing at all of the infant and nothing more of the minister than a proper intention.

Another of Cajetan's arguments based upon the mercy of God has fared no better with his critics. This, they say, is a line of reasoning that must be placed within the framework of revelation. To emphasize one of the elements of divine revelation to the neglect of others would be to distort God's word. Too much stress on the mercy of God would lead us to conclude that every human being *must* be saved; this universalist theory of salvation is not readily compatible with Christ's picture of the final judgment or with Paul's injunction that we work out our salvation in fear and trembling. God's mercy finds its expression in the elaborate plan of salvation that he has made known to us; a plan that embraces infant baptism. Although God is not bound to the details of this plan, we have no way of knowing, say Cajetan's critics, when and if God chooses to go beyond it.

Perhaps the most impressive of Cajetan's arguments is the

analogy he has drawn between the salvific faith of pre-Christian parents and the faith of a Christian mother and father. The faith of the pre-Christian world was enough to insure the child's salvation, and surely that faith was no more perfect than ours. May we not conclude therefore that the sacrament of nature is still available to us in an emergency? God alone knows the answer to that question, reply the critics; but it would seem that he has given us every indication that the answer is *no*. It is true that in every age of the world faith has been a constant salvific factor, a necessary link to God. It would seem too that in every age of the world there has been a symbol of faith that would bring into union with God the children who were incapable of an act of faith. Before the Jews there seems to have existed a sacrament of nature, the oblation that Cajetan described. This was succeeded by circumcision for Jewish males. God insisted on this rite if boys were to be incorporated into his chosen people. With the coming of Christ the ancient rites yielded to the sacrament of baptism. Now we cannot say for certain that Christ permitted the sacrament of nature to remain as an emergency alternative to baptism. On the contrary there seems to be evidence that he did not: ". . . unless a man be born again of water and the Spirit, he cannot enter into the kingdom of God" (John 3:5).

HERIS: A REVIVAL OF THE CAJETAN THEORY

Until recent years Cajetan's theory had been something of a theological fossil. Ten years ago it was revived and refurbished by the Dominican Ch.-V. Heris. After reviewing the official teaching of the Church, the French theologian concludes that baptism of water is necessary for infant salvation. He hastens to add, however, that the case of infants dying in the wombs of their mothers was not envisioned in the documents he examined. The Church has never defined that there is no way for them to reach salvation; at best this would be a theological conclusion drawn from the general teaching of the Church. Witness Trent's discussion of the theory of Cardinal Cajetan, and the council's refusal to condemn him. In Heris's opinion sacramental theology, and especially that of St. Thomas, would compel us to admit that salvation for these children is a definite possibility, thanks to the faith of their parents.

St. Thomas affirms that it is by faith and the sacraments of faith that we are united to Christ, incorporated in him, and made beneficiaries of the redemption.

> "The salvific power of Christ and his passion is applied to us by faith. . . . Men are delivered from sin especially by faith in his passion . . . The power of the sacraments, therefore, comes above all from faith in the passion of Christ."[16]

Infants presented for baptism are incapable of making an act of faith or of consenting in any way to the baptismal rite. How are they united to Christ by baptism? St. Thomas replies that spiritual generation effected in children by baptism resembles their physical generation in the wombs of their mothers. Children in the maternal womb, he says, take their nourishment from their mothers; just so infants who are, as it were, in the womb of mother Church receive their salvation not by their own personal acts but by those of the Church. They have the intention of receiving baptism, not by an act of their own will but by the act of those who present them for baptism.

In Thomas' evaluation of faith and the sacraments, Heris sees important consequences for the salvation of unbaptized infants. A catechumen, overtaken by death, can be saved by the faith which is implicit in his desire for baptism. Now we know, says Heris, that in the case of an infant, the faith of the parents stands good for that of the infant. If the infant should die prematurely, why would not that same faith, implicit in the parents' desire to baptize their child, obtain the infant's salvation? As Thomas remarks of pre-Christian parents, it was this faith in Christ to come that effected the salvation of their children.

Heris's position can be summed up in the following five propositions:

1. It is faith that gives a sacrament its value.
2. That faith can be simply the faith of the Church.
3. In infant baptism the faith of the Church and the faith of the parents insofar as they are members of the Church give the sacrament its value.
4. In baptism of desire faith suffices to sanctify the soul even without the reception of the sacrament.
5. In pre-Christian times the faith of the parents sufficed for the justification of their children. Would not that same faith be sufficient in the New Testament since it is now more perfect?

However forceful his presentation, Heris's conclusion is quite cautious: only the Church, he says, can declare in an absolute fashion that such children may indeed find their way to salvation.

Heris's critics have taken exception to his proposal on several counts. First of all, they say, his emphasis on the value of faith tends to obscure the difference between the sacraments of the Old Law and those of the New Testament. Under the

Old Law faith in Christ's passion, expressed by some external rite, was enough to justify a child. In the New Testament that faith justifies by *means* of the external rite, the sacrament. The sacraments of the New Testament confer grace *ex opere operato* independently of the works and merits of the minister and of the subject who receives them. As one of them worded it, "Faith gives the sacrament significance, it does not make it efficacious."[17] Faith links the sacrament to the passion of Christ, but it is from the passion that the efficacy of the sacrament flows.

These same critics suggest that Heris has made an unwilling ally of St. Thomas by failing to present a complete picture of his views of baptism of desire. Heris makes much of the fact that faith will at times justify a man without the visible sacrament of baptism. But as St. Thomas remarks, this is the case of a faith that is operative through charity. To say this is to take nothing away from faith; charity would be impossible without it. Nevertheless faith must be alive with charity if it is to bestow sanctifying grace. And while it is clear that a man can make an act of faith and charity for himself, it is not clear that he can do so for an infant dying without the sacrament of baptism. It is one thing to admit the possibility and quite another to concede the fact. Unless some evidence is forthcoming from the data of revelation, the critics conclude, Heris's theory remains highly conjectural.

MULDERS: UNCONSCIOUS DESIRE OF BAPTISM

Both Cajetan and Heris would extend the ordinary meaning of baptism of desire by having it include the desire of parents who wish to save their children. Approaching the problem from a different point of view, a Dutch Jesuit, Mulders, has suggested that infants might indeed be saved by baptism of desire, but the desire would be the unconscious desire mentioned by Pope Pius XII. Pius speaks of the divine invitation extended to all outside the Church to move from a state in which they cannot be sure of their eternal salvation. Although they are orientated toward (*ordinentur*) the Mystical Body of the Redeemer by a certain unconscious desire and *votum,* they lack, he says, much of the divine help which can be enjoyed only within the Church.

Mulders tries to push this "unconscious desire" back to an objective transformation that was effected in the child by the redemption. Man, says Mulders, is born into a supernatural order in which his intellective and volitional powers have been prepared for justification by the sacrifice of Christ. Every member of the race, he says, was baptized "germinally" in the death of Christ on Calvary. And in this orientation toward justification Mulders sees a "chance" of infant salvation.

Some of Mulders' critics are slow to evaluate his suggestions for fear that they have not fully grasped them. (Saiz.)[18] The elaboration of his suggestions which he promised has not yet appeared. As the theory stands, they say, it is vulnerable for its lack of evidence. Mulders must first demonstrate that the transformation he describes has actually taken place; secondly he must be prepared to prove that such a transformation may serve as baptism of desire. Until the Dutch theologian has managed to close these two gaps in his defense, his position is extremely vulnerable.[19]

ABBÉ BOUDES: THE DESIRE OF THE CHURCH

According to Cajetan and Heris baptism of desire is a way to salvation for unbaptized children, but the desire is that of

the child's parents. As Mulders sees it, the desire is an unconscious thing, an objective transformation effected in the child
by the redemptive sacrifice of Christ. The Abbé Boudes suggests another possibility. The desire is neither that of the child
nor of his parents but of the Church who thus continues her
role as the extension of Christ in the world. The Abbé bases
his theory on an analysis of Christ's role as the head of the
human race.

In his Epistle to the Romans St. Paul sets Christ and Adam
at opposite poles in human history, at the same time stressing
the fact that each of them represents the human race. Christ
emerges from this comparison as the victorious figure.
Through Adam sin and condemnation passed to mankind;
through Christ, however, justification comes to all. There is,
Paul insists, but one God, one mediator who has given himself
as a redemption for all.

The Abbé Boudes argues that this redemptive mission of
Christ consists essentially in uniting all creation to himself
as its center and head. At the culmination of Christ's work
the general resurrection of mankind serves to underscore the
bond that links all men to Christ. All will rise immortal on the
last day; no one will be excluded, not even the damned. "For
as in Adam all die, so in Christ all will be made to live" (1 Cor.
15:22). Since it is so evident, therefore, that no one can be
isolated from Christ, it is difficult to maintain, says Boudes,
that anyone at all dies with original sin on his soul. Limbo,
therefore, loses its reason for existing, and even unbaptized
children somehow find their way to heaven.

But how is original sin removed from the soul of an infant
who is incapable of any choice of his own? Boudes suggests
that the Church herself makes the choice for him. Pius XII
teaches that the Church continues on earth Christ's function

as mediator between God and men. Carrying on his sacerdotal work at the altar and through the sacraments, she strains every resource to insure the salvation of those committed to her charge. The baptism of an infant offers a perfect example of her concern and of her resources. Christ has revealed that faith is necessary for salvation, but an infant at the baptismal font is incapable of an act of faith. Is the child therefore lost? By no means, replies St. Augustine. The Church, he says, makes up with her own faith for what is lacking in the child. In this striking example of the Church's power the Abbé Boudes thinks that he may have found grounds of salvation for an unbaptized child. If the faith of the church is operative at a child's baptism, why may it not be operative at the death of an unbaptized child? If Boudes' theory is correct, the child would die with baptism of desire. The desire, however, would not be that of the child or his parents but of the Church herself.

Criticism of the Abbé Boudes centers on his use of the notion of solidarity. All of creation, says Boudes, is united to Christ as center and head; therefore, it is difficult to conceive of a single human being dying with original sin. His critics reply that there is between those two propositions a vast gulf which Boudes has failed to bridge. The idea of solidarity in Christ is both interesting and true, but it is also a vague idea. Its precise meaning must be spelled out before it can be used as the premise for a theory of infant salvation.

Boudes points out that an unbaptized child sharing in the resurrection is in some way bound to Christ. Theologians could easily admit this. But need that solidarity, they ask, imply anything more than the resurrection itself? Boudes thinks that it does. Others would disagree, and so the burden of the proof rests with Boudes.

The fact is that there are many degrees of solidarity with

Christ; and not all of them are effectively salvific. An adult might be linked to Christ by the characters of baptism, confirmation, holy orders, by the infused virtues of faith and hope, and yet live and die in the state of serious sin. The simple fact of a child's solidarity with Christ, therefore, does not itself guarantee his salvation. The point must be proven, not assumed; and this Boudes has not done, say his critics.

SAURAS: DEATH ITSELF A DESIRE OF BAPTISM

Death, as we mentioned, is the line of demarcation that separates the two main bodies of thought on infant salvation. With Emilie Sauras we approach this line of demarcation. His theory is something of a bridge between the two groups, since it includes elements of both. Sauras believes he can prove that death is itself a *votum* of baptism.

There is no doubt, says Sauras, that the desire for a sacrament is realized in an act of perfect charity. The question he asks is: Can this desire be realized in anything else? Can Christ give anything else so definite a relation to a sacrament that that thing becomes itself a desire for the sacrament? Not only is it within the power of Christ to do, replies Sauras; there is every evidence that this was indeed his will.

Crucial to the question, of course, is the notion of "desire for a sacrament" or, as theologians prefer to call it, the *votum sacramenti*. This *votum,* Sauras observes, can be either personal or real. The personal *votum* is a familiar thing, an act of the will by which we tend toward a thing, want to possess it. The catechumen who desires baptism has such a desire. But that desire, that tendency, can find expression in other ways as well. The inclination toward an object may exist in the thing itself; and this is called a *real* tendency (from the Latin *res:* "thing"). Things do possess a relation, or inclination, to other things, and this tendency may be called a *votum* or desire. Thus baptism itself is related to the blessed Eucharist in such a way that it may be called a desire (*votum reale*) of the Eucharist. It gives the baptized person a relation to the Blessed Sacrament even though he is himself incapable of human action. The reason for this is to be found in the nature of the sacraments of baptism and the Eucharist. The Eucharist is clearly the sacrament of life, and as such it is essential to salvation: "Unless you eat the flesh of the Son of man, and drink his blood, you shall not have life in you" (John 6:54). At the same time the Church teaches that baptism is not only necessary but sufficient for the salvation of an infant who never receives the Eucharist. The apparent conflict between these two facts is reconciled in the notion of baptism as a *votum reale* of the Eucharist.

Since Christ can quite clearly impress upon our actions an intention of his own, he could make the premature death of a child a *votum* of baptism. He chose to do this in the slaughter of the Innocents, when he made their deaths a *votum reale* of the sacrament. As Thomas Aquinas observed, Christ can confer the effects of a sacrament without the sacrament itself, if the sacrament is received *in voto*. According to Sauras, Christ has given such a sacramental destiny to some of men's actions. To preserve his Church he uses his power to confer the character of holy orders when the sacrament is invalidly administered. He has ordained martyrdom to achieve the effects of baptism or penance. He has made an act of perfect charity a *votum* of baptism—something it was not in the natural order of things, e.g. in Adam or Eve.

That Christ has in fact given this special character to the premature death of a child is suggested, says Sauras, by a consideration of Christ's salvific will and the necessity of baptism. The sincerity of Christ's salvific will is beyond cavil, says Sauras; it prompts him to give grace to those who do what lies within their power to effect their salvation. The premature death of an infant, however, offers an objection to Christ's salvific will which can be eliminated only if that death is itself a *votum reale* of baptism.

BRUNO WEBB: THE SACRAMENT OF DEATH

While Sauras sees death as an instrument of grace, an English Benedictine considers it a moment of decision. Dom Bruno Webb, like Abbé Boudes, prefaces his theory by exploring the solidarity of the human race in Christ and in Adam, for in the words of St. Augustine, "The whole human race is as it were two men, the First and the Second." Adam was not merely an individual man; he was first and foremost mankind itself already essentially complete. His sin, therefore, was the sin of Mankind. Thus, says Webb, when the first man lost the grace of innocence, the entire race was deprived of the supernatural life of grace. With the Second Adam the same principle holds true: Christ became in the order of redemption what Adam had been in the order of innocence. The Second Adam cannot be less perfect than the first; therefore his pledge to impart supernatural life to the whole body cannot be less universal than that of the first Adam would have been. "As in Adam all die," St. Paul said, "so in Christ all shall be made to live" (1 Cor. 15:22). But how does the grace of Christ reach an unbaptized infant?

Webb suggests that the death is itself the channel by which grace flows into the soul of the infant. A basic principle that seemingly underlies the whole order of the redemption, he says, is that God has transformed all penalty for sin into an instrument of expiation and of life; and death is the basic penalty for sin. In vitalizing death, the penalty of disobedience, with his own obedience unto death, Christ redeemed us by means of it. By consecrating death to God on Calvary, Christ transformed it into a quasi-sacrament, a channel of grace. Webb explains this quasi-sacramentality of death by employing an idea of St. Thomas Aquinas.

Thomas observed that once the soul is parted from the body the will is unchangeable. There must be an instant in death itself, therefore, when the will becomes changeless, when it either turns to God in perfect love or turns from him in complete malice; and at this moment the soul becomes saint or fiend. For the will to have acted with this entirety of its being, God must have enlightened the intellect both as to God's goodness and its own dispositions.

This view of death as a moment of decision does not envision infants alone, says Webb. Since the body has no place in this spirit choice, it is immaterial whether it be that of an adult or an infant. The necessity of such a choice is a universal law of mankind. Thus, in Webb's view, death is a channel of grace, a "quasi-sacrament," through which the Church is universally active in souls.

Both Webb and Sauras, of course, have encountered opposition on several scores. Their critics point out that the argument they have drawn from the solidarity of Christ and mankind is somewhat elusive. Webb, as we have seen, relies on the well-known text of St. Paul: "As in Adam all die, so in Christ all shall be made to live." Three scripture scholars, Allo, Prat and Spicq, concur in saying that Paul is speaking here of the resurrection of the just. Since Paul is apparently proclaiming the solidarity of Christ and those who have been reborn to the life of grace, there is no question in his text of those dying in original sin and still less of the impossibility of dying in this state. The critics, of course, concede a sort of bond even between the damned and Christ. As Thomas Aquinas observed centuries ago, all men rise from the dead because of Christ; the relation, however, is one of cause and effect. It is through the power of Christ that all men rise, even the damned, but only the just rise gloriously in imitation of their risen Lord. Thus there is a bond between Christ and every human being, even a child who dies unbaptized. Webb's critics would not readily admit, however, that the Lord demanded that each and every child be given a moment of grace in which to make an eternal choice.

Webb's basic principle is, as we have noted, that God has transformed all penalty for sin into an instrument of expiation. By his own death on Calvary Christ transformed the basic penalty for sin, human death, into an instrument of salvation. The death of an unbaptized child, Webb concludes, possesses an expiatory character and becomes a channel of grace. Critics might reply that death must indeed borrow its expiatory character from the death of Christ; but in order to do so some specific connection must be established between the death of the individual and that of Christ. Such a connection exists in the case of a martyr, as the Church has always taught. But it must be proved to exist elsewhere. Until this has been proven we must say that death retains its basic character of a sanction and not an expiation for sin.

Sauras' contribution to the problem was to make a child's death a *votum baptismi*. That Christ might have given this character to death is beyond question; that he chose to do so, says Sauras, is probable because of the sincerity of his salvific will. His critics would object that Sauras has a task to perform in proving that his *votum* has a real theological foundation, that it is baptism *in voto* as the Church understands it. The full implications of the salvific will of Christ are themselves highly debatable. By using a questionable interpretation of Christ's salvific will to corroborate an even more debatable theory Sauras leaves his entire thesis vulnerable to criticism.

GLORIEUX: THE MOMENT OF CHOICE

Possibly the most ingenious solution to this problem of an infant desire for baptism is one that can be erected on the hypothesis of the French theologian Glorieux. Actually Glorieux's speculations did not concern unbaptized infants at all but rather the moment of death and the possible implications of that moment. His ideas, however, lend themselves easily to the problem of unbaptized infants.[20]

Few concepts are more deeply rooted in Christian thought than the effects of death on the eternal destiny of man. All human activity properly speaking ends with death, and with it ceases the possibility of merit or demerit. There are no cogent reasons why this should be so, but God has indicated quite clearly that this is his will: "Night is coming, when no one can work." (John 9:4) There are moments of life given to man in which he can choose between God and himself; death, however, puts a decisive term to these moments of choice. For this reason the period of life and the period of merit are co-extensive. Glorieux's reflections begin at this point.

Does the instant of death itself, he asks, pertain to this life or to the next? If it is to be placed among the moments of this life, then it would seem that every human being has one final instant in which to choose between good and evil, between the selection and rejection of God. Glorieux's reasoning is tied to his analysis of this instant of death. Man can merit to the moment of death, but perhaps that moment is itself a moment of merit. If this can be shown to be so, the consequences would be immense indeed.

Death, Glorieux reminds us, is the separation of body and soul. Strictly speaking, it is the passage from one state to another that constitutes death, or the act of dying. The actual separation of soul and body is crucial to the notion of death. A man is alive so long as his soul is united to his body. The union may be tenuous and terribly fragile; so long as it remains, the man lives. When the union has been dissolved, when a separation of the two is effected, he is dead. The actual physical instant of death is the moment when the change is made from one state to another. This change is an instantaneous thing; the soul does not gradually leave the body the way water would seep from a broken vessel. The period of preparation for the moment of death may be more or less extensive as contact between body and soul is rendered more and more difficult. But when death occurs, it is instantaneous. As a result, the soul's leaving the body occupies the same physical instant as the soul's separation from the body. We might perhaps state this more clearly by saying that the last moment of life and the first moment of death are one and the same moment—and all because of the instantaneous character of death. Up to this point Glorieux's reflections seem a classic example of philosophical hair-splitting. The distinction he has made, however, has immediate and far-reaching consequences.

In the instant in which the soul is free of the body it begins immediately to exercise the intellectual and volitional activity that is normal to a disembodied spirit. It no longer depends upon the body for its knowledge; it is no longer influenced by the passions in the choices it makes. A wealth of intellectual and volitional activity is open to it. It retains, of course, all of the knowledge it quarried from creation during its sojourn on earth, but now its spiritual activity is totally untrammeled. It has an immediate and perlucid knowledge of itself, and consequently of its relation to its creator. With that knowledge a choice is possible between itself and its creator. Because a choice is the work of an instant, that choice may be compressed within the first instant of death, which, as we have seen, is the last instant of life. Is man to be given one final opportunity for salvation, therefore, at the instant of his death? A philosopher cannot answer that question, and so far Glorieux has played the role of the philosopher. As we have seen, there is no good reason why death must mark the end of man's period of probation. If it is so, it is because God wills it to be so: and here we enter the realm of revelation, the theologian's domain.

As a theologian Glorieux can now ask the question, Does man's period of probation end with death exclusively or inclusively? Does the instant of death itself with all its wealth of attendant activity also pertain to the period of probation, or is it excluded from exercising any influence on man's eternal destiny?

As a theologian must, Glorieux approaches the question by turning first to the Church. Her documents reveal no clear-cut decision in the matter, he says; consequently a theologian is free to suggest solutions, to construct hypotheses, so long as he knows these are always subject to her correction. With this as a premise Glorieux suggests that the instant of death itself does pertain to the period of probation, and this for three reasons. His hypothesis would best explain three problems that puzzle theologians: the obstinacy of the damned in evil, the disappearance of venial sin in the just after death, and the destruction of faith in the damned.

It is a strange fact, but true, that those in hell are eternally obdurate; we might, metaphorically, swing wide the gates of hell and no one would flee. The damned have made their choice, and they will cling to it eternally. This is understandable in the case of those fallen angels, the devils. Angels know by intuition, whereas man knows by reason, step by step. When angels make a decision their choice is prefaced by perlucid knowledge and an untrammeled will. Their minds do not fasten on first one facet and then another of a situation; their wills are not subject to the influence of passion, like human wills. Consequently when they have made a choice, there is no way of appealing the decision. There are no new motives that can be suggested, no new insights that can be offered; they have considered them all. There is nothing left to them, therefore, on which to base a new decision; their choice is eternal and irrevocable. God might, of course, give them some new insight, but this he refrains from doing; and left to themselves they cannot change.

Man presents quite a different problem. His final choice was that of a man, whose knowledge is less than comprehensive, whose will is subject to the assault of his passions. Why should he be eternally obdurate when he has been freed of emotion and begins to think as a disembodied spirit? Glorieux suggests that the answer may lie in his hypothesis. If the first instant of death does indeed pertain to the period of probation, a final human choice would be made under the same conditions and with the same eternal consequences as that made by the devils.

Glorieux suggests that his hypothesis would also explain the disappearance of venial sin among the just in the next life. Venial sin, of course, implies some fault and entails some punishment; and neither may remain if the just soul is to enter heaven. The sanction is inflicted in purgatory; and theologians say that an act of charity will remove the fault. Here, however, we have a difficulty. When is this act of charity to be performed: in this life or in the next? If the Glorieux hypothesis is tenable, then that act of charity would be found in the first instant of death, when the soul moves toward its creator in an act of love.

One final question is answered by the Glorieux hypothesis —the disappearance of faith in the damned. Since faith is a theological virtue, there is no likelihood that it would remain in a soul in hell. But that leaves a theologian the task of explaining its destruction. Faith is destroyed by a sin against faith. But a soul may damn itself for a dozen different reasons and never sin against faith. If the soul were to make an effective choice against God in the instant of death, however, its choice would be a total thing, a complete aversion of mind and will. Consequently not only charity and hope would disappear but faith as well.

The Glorieux theory was born of philosophical speculation and bolstered by theological reasoning. And although it was not originally intended as a way of salvation for unbaptized infants, his hypothesis has an obvious application to the problem. At the instant of death, the child would begin immediately to exercise the rich intellectual and volitional life of a disembodied soul. Since that moment of death would pertain to his period of probation, he could choose his eternity. He would have an immediate and transparent knowledge of himself and of his relation to his creator. Knowing himself, he would of course love himself; he would be free to subject that self-love to his creator or he could prefer it to God. The choice would determine his eternity.

What criticism might be offered to Glorieux? First of all, it would seem difficult to criticize him on purely philosophical grounds. His hypothesis is closely reasoned; his distinction subtle but apparently valid. Most theologians do shy away from the theory, however, and their most telling argument is drawn from the common view of man's period of probation on earth.

The period of probation is defined not merely by the union of body and soul but by the acts of a man, not a disembodied spirit. Consequently the physical moment of death and the final moment of life may well be one and the same, but no eternal consequence might be deduced from this. The period of probation embraces so many moments of time, but even more to the point it is a period of truly human activity; and a disembodied spirit is not a man. He is one potentially; and he will be one again when his soul is reunited to his body in the resurrection, but until then his actions are not human in the accepted sense of the word. Once the human composite has been dissolved, the period of probation is at an end, and Glorieux's speculations become pointless. This criticism is not completely persuasive, but it does show why Glorieux's theory must, for the present at least, remain a hypothesis, a tentative solution to a problem.[21]

LAURENGE: DECISION AFTER DEATH

If death is a line of demarcation between the two sets of theories we have so far discussed, it is also a boundary beyond which salvation theories seldom venture. There is a minority view, however, which claims that the only solution to the problem of unbaptized infants lies beyond the grave. Henri Klee pioneered the idea in the nineteenth century, and it has found advocates in our own time in the persons of M. Laurenge and Vincent Wilkin.

Laurenge builds his thesis on the familiar ground of God's

salvific will. Given the sincerity of his salvific will, argues
Laurenge, God must furnish every infant a means of salvation;
and he has not done this simply by instituting the sacrament of
baptism. Baptism is a physical impossibility in so many cases
that perhaps two-thirds of the race would be beyond its reach.
Theologians, it is true, would argue that God has done all that
his justice demands when he prepares the instrument of salvation; he need not see to it that it is available in every case.
They distinguish too between means that are proximately and
remotely sufficient for salvation. To Laurenge's way of thinking, however, they are playing with words. There is a correla-
tion, he insists, between the reality of God's salvific will and
the reality of the steps he has taken to insure that salvation is
at least physically possible. A child for whom baptism is a
physical impossibility has not been given the means to save his
soul in this life; God, who truly wills the child's salvation,
would, therefore, provide him with a means of salvation after
death.

Catholic doctrine, of course, teaches that men cannot merit
after death, that heaven and hell are eternal, and that there is
no passage from the one to the other. The doctrine is summed
up in the scriptural formula: "Night is coming, when no one
can work" (John 9:4). It is true, says Laurenge, that innumer-
able passages of Scripture urge us to live in such a way that
death finds us prepared for heaven. It is no less true, he insists,
that these passages from Scripture envision adults who are capable of meriting heaven; to apply the words of Scripture to infants who are incapable of choice would be to overextend the
text and to abuse its meaning. Revelation leaves no doubt that
an adult must save his soul before death if he is to save it at all.
Only by doing violence to revelation, however, could we apply
the same maxim to an infant who had no opportunity to merit.

Denied their moment of merit in life, these children will find it after death; there, succored by the grace of God, they can freely choose their final end. How this will be Laurenge explains by bringing into play a theory of St. Thomas Aquinas.

When a man begins to use his intelligence, says Thomas, he reflects according to his capacities upon himself and upon his destiny. If at that moment he turns toward his final end, he obtains the remission of original sin; if he fails to do so, he sins seriously. There may be some doubt, says Laurenge, that such a choice is psychologically necessary at the dawn of intellectual life; there is no doubt that some such choice is necessary for a child who dies unbaptized.

When the child's intelligence awakens after death, God gives it the grace to orientate itself toward its final goal. If the grace is efficacious, the child is saved; if it is a merely sufficient grace, the child freely turns from his final end and damns himself to hell.

In the course of his exposition Laurenge faces up to two obvious difficulties. One of these is the problem he finds in a decision of the Council of Florence:

> "The souls of those who die in actual mortal sin or
> in original sin alone go down to hell to be punished
> by different penalties."[22]

In a lengthy appendix to his article Laurenge sets out to prove that Florence meant only to reproduce the Council of Lyons; and Lyons, he says, had no intention of defining the eternal damnation of unbaptized children.

Another problem discussed by Laurenge is that posed by the Church's teaching on the necessity of baptism. This necessity, he says, must be interpreted within the total content of Christian revelation; and here the salvific will of God is our guide. Martyrdom and the act of perfect charity are limitations on the necessity of baptism; so is the salvific will of God. Baptism is not so necessary that a man cannot be saved by martyrdom or by an act of perfect charity; nor is it so necessary that it overrides the salvific will of God.

CRITICISM

Of all the salvation theories we have discussed, that of Laurenge has been met with the greatest reservations. One author labels it "heretical."[23] F. Cayré, the editor of *L'Année Théologique,* in which the Laurenge article first appeared, prefaced it with the remark that it seemed to run contrary to the whole of Christian tradition. Lopez Martinez feels that it is false, gratuitous, and irreconcilable with Catholic doctrine.[24]

Much of Laurenge's thesis, it is charged, rests on a purely negative premise: his theory has not been condemned by the Church. However this may be, say his critics, the author must still take a very long stride from the possible to the factual; and his whole argument is based on a debatable interpretation of God's salvific will. Any discussion of this salvific will in its application to infants moves necessarily in something of a fog; and Laurenge's opponents would be the first to admit it. They maintain nonetheless that one fact at least is clear: God's salvific will is not absolute but conditioned. It is conditional upon the free will of man. To their way of thinking it is also conditioned in the case of a child by the will of the child's parents and even by the forces of nature. A parent's lack of co-operation or even the interference of some natural cause may check God's salvific will as effectively as the free choice that sends a man to hell.

Now this explanation of God's salvific will is not entirely persuasive, but neither is it an exercise in minor logic. Because of its basis in tradition and the number of theologians it has impressed over the centuries it demands a hearing. To insist as Laurenge does that God's salvific will must overrule both the will of the parents and the forces of nature is to take a position that requires more evidence than Laurenge has mustered.

At least one critic believes that Laurenge has overstated the problem posed for him by the Council of Florence. Laurenge seems to fear that his opponents would argue that Florence had defined the eternal situation of unbaptized infants. This is not the case, as most theologians would readily admit. Florence was concerned with settling the old dispute on the immediate character of a reward or sanction after death; and the entire emphasis in its definition is placed here. Laurenge's basic difficulty lies elsewhere. He must come to grips with the apparent conviction of the Church that there is no salvation without baptism in this life. Until he has met and somehow resolved this difficulty he is not really free to move on to his theory of merit after death.

Laurenge's thesis has the advantage of clearing up a host of difficulties that surround God's salvific will, since it places responsibility for infant salvation squarely in the hands of the children. But it also places the fate of infants in a new and disturbing perspective, in which we see them confronted with a choice between heaven and hell, eternal damnation and the beatific vision. The decisive element in their choice is the grace of God; for some the grace will be efficacious, for others it will be merely sufficient. Here, as A. Michel remarks, we have the mystery of God's predilection, but in the circumstances it takes on a truly tragic aspect. The theory certainly does away with limbo, but it can bring little consolation to parents who realize its full implications.

VINCENT WILKIN: SALVATION IN
THE FINAL RESURRECTION

The English Jesuit Vincent Wilkin agreed with Laurenge in looking beyond death for a solution to the problem of the unbaptized infant. In his opinion, however, their salvation will not be a matter of choice or merit but rather the result of their recapitulation in Christ in the resurrection of the dead.

Once a person is dead, says Wilkin, the time of trial is over. There can be no further act of his own will which will determine his destiny. This is true not only of the damned but of unbaptized children as well. There can be no question, therefore, of a choice with eternal consequences for those beyond the grave.

At the resurrection of the dead, however, original sin will be destroyed, Satan will lose his hold on the human race, and unbaptized children will find the way to heaven open to them. The reason for all this is to be found in the place the resurrection holds in the redemptive plan of God. On that final day the whole body of mankind will be assembled, that corporate man whom God wished to save and whom Christ set out to redeem. And it will be then that the redemptive work of Christ will find its fulfillment, for the resurrection takes place on the same level and with the same universality as original sin; it has the same coverage as death. Death, Wilkin observes, is not just a biological fact but an enemy of God, representing as it does the sin of the world. Death was the penalty of original sin, and the resurrection by its very nature signifies the end of original sin.

There are several ways in which original sin may be said to cease when mankind rises from the dead. The first of these is the completeness of the human race; no new subjects will fall heir to original sin, for Adam will have no new posterity.

Moreover, original sin will lose the hold which it has on the race, a hold secured by two factors: the power of Satan over the race and relation of the race to Adam. Satan has been able to introduce death into a race never intended by God to die. On the final day, however, he will be powerless to impose death on the living, and incapable of maintaining its hold on the dead. His power will have been broken by the power of Christ. At the same time, original sin will lose the claim it had on the race through Adam, for Adam will no longer be the head of the race; his position will have been taken by Christ. On that final day the race to which all men had belonged will have expired, not statistically but institutionally. The old race sprung from Adam will be dead; the new race reborn in the resurrection will be recapitulated entirely under the headship of Christ. And it is in this recapitulation that a solution can be found for the problem of unbaptized children.

Can unbaptized children, Wilkin asks, continue in a state of original sin when original sin itself has been abolished, when the whole economy of original sin has been wiped away? The child has lost its solidarity with Adam and has escaped the power of Satan. At this point Wilkin argues that an unbaptized child must go to heaven. There are only four things, he points out, that could keep the infant from God; the will of God, the will of Satan, the will of Adam, the child's own will. None of them are obstacles to infant salvation. God wills their salvation; the will of Satan, like that of Adam, is no longer operative; and the child's own will is incapable of acting at all. The child, therefore, must go to heaven. The question remains: How does the child get the sanctifying grace necessary for salvation? Father Wilkin suggests that the removal of original sin is one of the effects of a universal baptism that takes place on the last day.

Christ insisted on the necessity of rebirth if one is to enter the kingdom of heaven. But the resurrection of the dead, Wilkin says, is a rebirth. St. Augustine observed that St. Paul called the resurrection not only a rebirth but an adoption of sons, a redemption. In other words it is not only a physical act of rebirth but also a communication of supernatural life by which a person reborn is also a son of God. In Wilkin's view the teaching of St. Paul seems to demand that the resurrection of the dead be accompanied by an outpouring of grace that will manifest the pre-eminence of Christ over Adam.

In Romans 5:15 St. Paul claims that the grace of Christ is even more effective than the sin of Adam: "For if by the offense of the one the many died, much more has the grace of God, and the gift in the grace of the one man Jesus Christ, abounded unto the many." Wilkin points out the difficulty that arises from a comparison of the monstrous inequality that exists between those who died in Adam and of those who profit by the death of Christ. Some, he admits, solve the problem by emphasizing the potential of Christ's merits, stressing their power to justify every man who accepts the grace of Christ. But if infants are not saved by the merits of Christ, Wilkin observes, then the potential of these merits becomes an academic question and the salvific power of Christ suffers in comparison with the lethal power of Adam.

The pre-eminence of Christ's redemptive work must be vindicated, and it can be, says Wilkin, if there is a flow of grace to the entire race corresponding to the coverage of death. "It would not be necessary for that grace to be accepted or to take effect universally, because its refusal would not be due to Adam's sin but to a new and separate act of a human will in the similitude of Adam's sin. But it would be required that the grace be there and available to every member of the race that fell in Adam. It would thus be in efficacy as broadly racial as the effects of disobedience in Adam."[25] Therefore, on the last day of complete and fulfilled redemption, the grace of Christ goes out seeking to embrace all individuals.

Wilkin hastens to add that this flood of grace fails to affect the damned. By individual act they have set themselves apart from humanity as a whole. Grace and love do flow out even to the damned at the moment of resurrection, but they prefer to remain in their sin. Thus the fulfillment of redemption on the last day does not interfere with the final decision of the damned to reject God.

The case of an unbaptized child, however, is different. As he does not reject the grace of Christ, he is justified and goes to heaven. His history, says Wilkin, has been brief, marked by complete passivity and ignorance. After a short life he dies and will be born again. He will be created anew so that, while remaining himself, he is now a son of God. He continues to embody the state of the race, but it is no longer a fallen race but one redeemed by Christ. And his rebirth is a kind of baptism. For what, asks Wilkin, is baptism except a rebirth in the Spirit and a vital union with Christ? Those who are reborn in Christ on the last day are united with him in his resurrection; and all, except the obdurate, go to heaven for all eternity.

In Wilkin's view, therefore, children go to limbo, but only to find that limbo is the "baptistry of heaven." They participate in the resurrection of Christ along with the rest of mankind, and there is nothing in them to prevent the supernatural efficacy of the resurrection taking place. They remain the passive embodiments of the human race. But the race is no longer fallen; it is redeemed. That redemption these unbaptized children show forth in themselves.

To date only one review of Wilkin's book has appeared in the professional journals; and the review was not unfavorable. Writing in *Theological Studies,* Father Kilmartin, S.J., observed that critics might take issue with the author's interpretation of Scripture; nonetheless, he continued, if a solution is to be found to the perplexing problem of unbaptized children, it will most likely be in the area explored by Wilkin.[26]

Any criticism of Wilkin's thesis must necessarily be somewhat reserved. The book was published posthumously and, as its editor remarked: "This is not the book Wilkin wished to write." If death had not intervened, the author might well have forestalled the objections that will certainly be raised against his thesis. As it is, the book is necessarily open to certain criticisms.

Those who read *From Limbo to Heaven* are sure to remark that the author failed to cope with the major obstacle to his theory—the apparent conviction of the Church through the centuries that a child must be baptized in this life if it is to enter the kingdom of heaven. This idea is not a dogma of the Church; it has never been the object of a definition. But it is a persuasion that seems to have accompanied the thinking of the Church over the centuries. And a theologian must somehow evaluate this persuasion before he can move on to propose a theory of salvation that takes place beyond the grave. Otherwise, his theorizing remains vulnerable, however attractive it may be. And Wilkin's theory is attractive; it explores in an interesting way the implications of the solidarity of the human race in Christ.

Thomas Aquinas and Suarez would find nothing unfamiliar in the notion of solidarity between Christ and the world of the unbaptized infant. St. Thomas saw Christ as the efficient cause of the general resurrection; and in this sense his triumph includes even infants. Suarez envisioned the children of limbo paying homage to Christ their prince, honoring him for their share in his triumph, a life of human perfection. Each of these suggestions embodies a degree of solidarity with Christ. Neither implies the salvation of the child. The fact of solidarity between infant and redeemer is not itself a guarantee, therefore, that a child will find its way into the kingdom of heaven. A very special union with Christ must be established if the relationship is to be effectively salvific.

"There must be a solution somewhere," writes Wilkin; "if these unbaptized children are not saved, then clearly Adam's power over the race is more effective than Christ's. If these children are not saved, then in the conflict between Christ and Satan, the unbaptized would stand as an eternal victory for Satan over Christ."[27]

We might contrast these words of Wilkin with those of the Council of Trent:

"Even though Christ dies for all, not all received the benefit of his passion. But those to whom he communicated it."[28]

The salvific power of Christ's redemptive work is capable of reaching everyone; as a matter of fact it does not seem to reach all. We are in the presence here of a problem far more perplexing than that posed by an unbaptized child—the mystery of predestination. Ours is not the best of all possible worlds. If it were, each of Adam's children would be given nothing but efficacious grace and thus save his soul. The hell that was created for the devil and his angels would have remained for-

ever closed to the human race. Nevertheless hell remains a
possibility for every human being. Christ's description of the
last judgment leads us to believe that some men at least will be
damned; and we are warned by God to work out our salvation
in fear and trembling. This situation need not have been, God
might have arranged that Christ's triumph be universally efficacious; apparently he decided otherwise. Some will be lost
who might have been saved. And although it is true that they
freely chose their damnation, it is equally true that God might
have seen to it that they freely cast their lot with Christ. This
is the mystery of predestination. It is a problem of predilection
whose solution lies in the depths of the Godhead.

Theologians have striven for centuries to reconcile the fact
of predestination with the triumph of Christ. Their solution is
that of the Council of Trent. Christ died for all but not all
profited by his death, only those to whom he communicated
the benefits of his passion. According to theologians, the sincerity of God's salvific will remains intact because God gives
each man sufficient grace to save his soul. Christ's triumph is
more than equal to Adam's failure because Christ's merits
were more than enough to save the entire race. As a matter of
fact they do not bring corporate mankind intact into the kingdom of God. His merits might have done so; that their potential is not realized is not only the result of man's choice, it is
the choice of God. And this, as we have said, is the mystery of
predestination. St. Augustine grappled with the problem for
most of his days; perhaps this accounts for his lack of dismay
at seeing an unbaptized child excluded from the beatific vision.

Nor is Wilkin beyond criticism when he states that the
unbaptized infant would stand as an eternal victory for Satan
over Christ. As we shall see, the prominent Swiss theologian
Charles Journet, in company with Suarez, shows how even the

children in limbo might share in the victory of their redeemer. In his view they are saved, but their salvation is not union with Christ in heaven but rather the restoration to their human nature of what it lost in Adam.

CONCLUSION

The somewhat bewildering complex of theories that we have seen lend weight to Fernandez's observation that the problem of unbaptized children is not one but many; and the difficulties vary from case to case. Cajetan's suggestions, for instance, offer no solution to the problem of a child whose parents may be completely unaware of Christ and his redemptive work. Nor would it prove of any use in a case where the parents were indifferent to the salvation of their children. If we are to view the problem in all its complexity, therefore, we must with Fernandez distinguish at least five possible cases:

1. Jewish children dying before they could be circumcised, or even before the institution of this "quasi-sacrament."
2. Pagan children who died before the coming of Christ.
3. Children dying today in a region where Christ is unknown.
4. Children dying in the wombs of their mothers.
5. Children of Christian parents who die before they can be baptized.

The first two cases present comparatively slight difficulty for theologians, who readily admit the existence of the sacrament of nature.

The last three cases, however, present quite a different picture; as the theologian moves from the third case to the fifth, he encounters increasingly formidable obstacles. Of these three situations the one most accessible to a solution is that of the child dying today in a region where Christ is unknown. Here many of the pitfalls that confront the theorist can be avoided. While paying full homage to the law of baptism he can confine his investigation to the question of fact: Has the law of baptism *de facto* been universally promulgated? Or is it conceivable that regions do exist where the primitive rite of nature still obtains? Theologians are less reluctant to concede ground here than they would be in the final two cases.

Gerson was the first to propose the possibility of salvation for a child dying in the womb of its mother. Biel and Cajetan followed, and in time their ideas have been endorsed or refined by Beni and Santos. The distinguished theologian Lercher, too, had his reservations about including these infants under the general law of baptism.[29]

The most serious objections, however, are reserved for the final category of problems posed by unbaptized infants—the children of Christian parents. And it is here that the liberal theologians—if we may use that ambiguous term—face the gravest difficulties in tradition and in the teaching of the Church. What these problems are and what steps these theologians have taken to resolve them, we will see in the following chapter.

V

Contemporary Debate

Even a cursory reading of the current literature makes it clear that the theologians engaged in the present debate are divided on five fundamental issues:

1. The necessity of baptism for infant salvation.
2. The death in original sin of unbaptized infants.
3. The existence of limbo.
4. The salvific will of God.
5. The possibility for infants of baptism of desire.

Conservative theologians insist that God's salvific will finds its expression in the sacramental system. The sacrament of baptism, they say, is necessary for salvation; and since an infant is incapable of baptism of desire, his need of the sacrament is absolute and unqualified. When such a child dies unbaptized, God's salvific will ceases to be operative for him; and he spends his eternity in limbo.

Liberal theologians have challenged their conservative colleagues to reappraise the five propositions on which they have erected their thesis. The ensuing discussion has moved across areas that embrace a vast amount of history and theology. And if this chapter is not to become a book, we can do no more than sketch the terrain. Of the five issues in question the most fundamental and the most troublesome is that of the necessity of baptism.

THE NECESSITY OF BAPTISM FOR SALVATION: A—THE CHURCH'S TEACHING

Although the Church has repeatedly spoken of the necessity of baptism for salvation, she gave the idea its most definitive expression in the documents of the Council of Trent; and it is to these that we will first turn our attention. They are doubly interesting because they were formulated at a time when Cardinal Cajetan's theory of infant salvation was being debated by the Fathers of the council.

The Council of Trent and the Necessity of Baptism

On May 21, 1546, the question of original sin, its nature and remedy, was brought before the council for consideration. Some of the bishops favored a simple reaffirmation of the decisions of earlier councils. The majority disagreed, however, feeling that the ideas of the Protestant Reformers demanded a more vigorous response. The Anabaptists, one of the Protestant sects, refused to baptize their children, saying that the child had neither the faith that was required for the sacrament nor the reason necessary to ratify what was done in his name. Since they denied the existence of original sin, they could see little point in infant baptism. The Swiss reformer Zwingli admitted that the sacrament was necessary for incorporation into the people of God but denied that it was required for salvation. Calvin taught that an infant draws his sanctification from his origin of Christian parents. It was in the context of this new Protestant theology that the Council of Trent took its stand on baptism, and especially on the importance of the sacrament for the remission of original sin and for justification.

Baptism and Original Sin

In June of 1546 theologians formulated the first draft of a statement on original sin and submitted it to the council. A good many additions and changes were suggested before the statement took the form finally adopted by the bishops of Trent. After reaffirming the traditional Catholic belief in the existence of original sin (Canon 2), the bishops stated that the only remedy for original sin is the merit of Christ applied to infants and adults by the sacrament of baptism (Canon 3). In a fourth canon the council defined three propositions:

1. A newborn child must be baptized (here the bishops had the Anabaptists in mind).
2. The child must be baptized to obtain the remission of original sin and eternal life (a statement directly contrary to Zwingli, Calvin, and the Anabaptists).
3. The child must be baptized even if it be born of baptized parents (against Calvin).[1]

The following January the bishops took up the question of justification and returned to the sacrament of baptism. Justification, they said, was man's transferal from his condition as a son of Adam to a state of grace and divine adoptive sonship. And this divine adoption, the bishops continued, was effected by the sacrament of baptism or by desire for it (*votum baptismi*). What is more, if men are not reborn in Christ, they are never justified.[2]

In these propositions the bishops of Trent recapitulated

centuries of Catholic thought on original sin, justification, and
the relation of these two facts to baptism. Climaxing months
of discussion, they were the most authoritative statements ever
issued by the teaching authority of the Church on the necessity
of the sacrament for salvation. It was at this point that the salvation theories of Cardinal Cajetan were brought before the
council.

The Question of Cardinal Cajetan

A few days after the council had adopted the decrees of the
sixth session, the bishops submitted to the theologians for criticism a number of propositions which they considered to be
suspect. For some reason the theologians went beyond their
agenda, however, and began to discuss the possible salvation of
children who die without baptism. One of the theologians, An-
drew de Vega, suggested that the following proposition should
be condemned:

"Children who die without baptism may be saved."[3]

Another theologian, Leoninus, suggested condemning the idea
that children could be baptized in the womb.[4] Although baptism *"in utero"* is an accepted practice today, it was once the
subject of much theological speculation. Part of the reason for
this, of course, was the primitive state of medical science; but
there were theological considerations as well. Christ had said
that a man must be reborn if he were to enter the kingdom of
God; but how could he be born again if he had not been born
at all? A child still in the womb seemed to be excluded even
from the possibility of baptism. From the suggestion made by
Leoninus, we can see that the problem still occupied the attention of sixteenth-century theologians. In the opinion of many

of them baptism was impossible for a child in the womb. And it was just such a child that Cardinal Cajetan chose to discuss in his famous theory of infant salvation. The case was an ideal springboard for the cardinal's speculations, juxtaposing as it did the notions of the necessity of baptism and God's salvific will in a situation where a child was simply beyond the reach of the sacrament. The celebrated history of Cajetan's theory prompts us to let the cardinal describe it for himself:

> "Children who die in the womb of their mother can be saved, (as we have said above of those infants who die before it is possible to administer baptism to them) . . . They can be saved, I say, by the sacrament of baptism received not really, but *'in voto'* [by the desire] of their parents [who would give] a blessing to the infants and invoke the Trinity.
>
> "Two reasons prompted me to come to this conclusion. First of all, it is proper that the divine mercy provide for the salvation of men in every natural condition, in such a way that in whatever state man may be found, he could not allege the impossibility of salvation. Now that impossibility would exist for an infant dying in the womb of his mother if the faith of his parents could not save him.
>
> "In [the womb] the infant is capable of receiving baptism of blood; if a child yet enclosed in the womb of his mother could receive death for Christ, he would be a martyr as are the holy innocents. It is then reasonable to admit that the faith of his parents could produce the same result as suffering borne by infants.

"Thus then one would be acting prudently and wisely in the case where children come to die in the womb of their mothers, whether because of the mother's sickness or a difficulty in birth, in giving the children a blessing with the invocation of the Sovereign Judge. Who can say the divine mercy would not accept that baptism received by the desire of the parents. This embraces no contempt of the sacrament, since it is the impossibility of the sacrament which forces parents to have recourse to it."

Cardinal Cajetan and the Bishops of Trent

For thirteen days the Fathers of Trent cast their ballots for or against the condemnation of the following proposition:

"Children in the wombs of their mothers can be saved by blessing and the invocation of the Trinity."

Cajetan's name was not mentioned in the proposition, but the wording of the theory and the subsequent debate made it clear that the cardinal himself was under fire.

Fifty-five votes were cast. Twenty-six of these asked for a condemnation of the proposition. Six others asked for its condemnation but with reservations. Some of these reservations were such that the bishops actually were condemning an idea other than Cajetan's. Three of the bishops suggested condemning the idea of certain salvation for the children—something Cajetan himself might have agreed to since he spoke only of the *possibility* of God's intervention. The remaining bishops, twenty-one in number, either abstained from voting on a condemnation or else came to Cajetan's defense.[5]

Seripando, the distinguished General of the Augustinian Order, marshalled a number of arguments in defense of his old teacher:[6]

1. If Cajetan's proposition is condemned, it would follow that the faith of the people of the Old Testament was of more value than ours for, as Gregory says: what the waters of baptism do for us, faith effected for the people of the Old Testament.

2. Cajetan's theory deals with a case where the administration of baptism is impossible. If his theory is untenable, then God has made, it would seem, an impossible demand upon men, insisting on baptism even when it cannot be administered.

3. The power of God which had not before been restricted would now be confined to the sacramental system; he could not act independently of the sacraments which he has instituted.

4. There would be a normal human condition in which man could exist without any means of saving his soul.

5. In conclusion, Seripando remarked on Cajetan's observation that he dealt with a case where all care had been exercised, where there was no neglect, but only the simple impossibility of administering the sacrament.

The Dominican General, Francis Romaeus, came to Cajetan's defense with the observation that the cardinal had proposed his ideas as a theory, subject to correction. His own opinion was that as a theory it should not be condemned; it was too well-reasoned to warrant it.[7]

On February 22nd, 1547, the Secretary of the Council, Massarelli, summed up the long discussion of Cajetan's theory. Some, he said, suggested condemning the idea that the children under discussion will certainly be saved. Others would condemn the thought that every child of this sort is as certainly saved as though he had been baptized.

Clearly, then, the bishops showed great hesitation in condemning Cajetan's suggestions for infant salvation. At no time did as many as half the bishops vote for its condemnation. Indeed, some very distinguished members of the council came to his defense. These facts may explain the subsequent turn of events.

The original list of errors submitted to the council was sent back to the theologians for revision; on February 26th the list was revised and again submitted to the bishops; Cajetan's theory was no longer on the list. The reason given for the omission was that "it did not pertain to the teaching on baptism."[8] As we have seen, the bishops of the council were clearly divided on the question of condemnation. Perhaps they hesitated to condemn so distinguished a churchman at this critical period in the history of the Church. Probably too the defense of Cajetan conducted by the generals of the Augustinian and Dominican orders had convinced the council that Cajetan's idea was not entirely without its merits. However this may be, the majority of the bishops present at the council were content with their solution to the problem of Cajetan. Four men who demanded that Cajetan's proposition be restored to the list of errors were immediately answered by four others who came to the cardinal's defense. Among the four defenders were two who earlier had voted for the condemnation of Cajetan's theory. The votes for condemnation were now so much in the minority that Cajetan's theory was eliminated decisively from the list of errors.[9]

The assertion has often been made that Cajetan's theory of infant salvation was excised from his works by order of Pope Pius V; the inference is that the pope disapproved of the theory although the council did not. As a matter of fact the passage in question was eliminated from the edition of Cajetan's commentary on St. Thomas, but the decision seems to have been entirely that of the editor; there is no solid historical evidence that Pius V had any influence on the decision.

Cajetan's Theory vs. the Necessity of Baptism

The Council of Trent taught that baptism was necessary for infant salvation while at the same time it tolerated the salvation theory of Cajetan. The two decisions are not contradictory, nor even inconsistent. "Necessity" is a broad term admitting of many shades of meaning. When God commanded Elias to cross the desert, the prophet felt it necessary to act; and the necessity had its origins in a divine command. This is what theologians would term a necessity of precept. Forty days and nights of walking across the desert make it crashingly clear that Elias' legs were also a necessity if he were to carry out the divine command. And this was a necessity of a different, more urgent, sort. His legs were the means, the instruments of his journeying; and we would say that they were necessary with a necessity of means. Still, it is conceivable that the prophet might have made the journey without the use of his legs, for there were horses and chariots even in those primitive days. If an instrument is so necessary, however, that there is no substitute for it, then the necessity of means is said to be absolute. This situation may be grounded either in a divine decree or in the nature of the thing itself. Had Elias been commanded to walk across the desert, his legs would have been absolutely necessary, but only because of a divine command; for there were, as we said, other ways of making the journey. The relation of means to end, however, may be so intimate and so urgent that it would exist independently of any precept. If a man has no eyes, he cannot see; if a man is not justified, he is incapable of the beatific vision. A necessity of this sort admits neither substitutes nor exceptions.

In his commentary on St. Thomas, Cardinal Cajetan explored the necessity of baptism, looking for some way to salvation for children who were beyond the reach of the sacrament. God, he felt sure, would not impose a precept that was impossible of fulfillment, for his justice would not allow him to make unreasonable demands. Yet this would indeed be the case, thought the cardinal, if children in the womb must be baptized. They could not obey the divine command, even though they were living in the most normal human condition—that of a child in its mother's womb. Since God would not demand the impossible of any human being, thought Cajetan, there must be some other way for these children to reach salvation. If they themselves are incapable of the faith that is the beginning of salvation, then perhaps the faith of their parents might take its place.

Apparently the bishops of Trent did not think that Cajetan's theory collided with their own teaching on the necessity of baptism, for they refused to condemn him. But the reason, which we have noted, that they gave for their action was somewhat cryptic: "[The theory] does not pertain to the teaching on baptism."

"It does not pertain. . . ."

Various explanations have been offered of this curious phrase in the Tridentine verdict. One theologian, Ruch, said that it was Trent's way of remaining noncommittal, neither condemning nor approving the cardinal's proposition.[10] More recently Heris offered another explanation. What the council meant, he said, was that Cajetan's idea was so little opposed to the conciliar teaching on baptism that it did not warrant further discussion.[11] Obviously the validity of these interpretations can be measured only by recalling the "teaching" of the council itself.

Three things become clear from a reading of Trent's deliberations during the months of 1546-1547: (1) When Trent defined the necessity of baptism for infants, it was speaking of a general, not an absolute, necessity. (2) Its definition was prompted by the Reformers who disputed the necessity of the sacrament even to the point of refusing to baptize their children. (3) The infants in question were the "newly-born," not the infants *"in utero"* of Cajetan's theory. These three factors, I believe, explain why the bishops of Trent declined to condemn Cajetan without prejudice to their decrees on baptism: his theory was outside the scope of their deliberations.

General Necessity of Baptism

When the council in its fifth session decreed that the sacrament of baptism was necessary for the remission of original sin even in the newborn infant, it did not preclude the possibility of the sin being removed by some other agency. Had it done so, it would have flown in the face of one of the most ancient traditions of the Church—the belief that even an infant can be a martyr. When the bishops then were asked to condemn Cajetan for suggesting that still another salutary agency might be operative in the case of infants, they declined to do so; and their refusal in no way compromised what they had stated in their earlier decrees. According to Trent the sacrament of baptism was a necessary means of removing original sin; but the council had not pronounced it so necessary that it left the child no possible alternative.

Trent and the Reformers

A second factor in Trent's verdict on the Cajetan issue was the historical context of its decrees on baptism. The entire matter of original sin, justification, and baptism was under review precisely because it had been challenged by the Reformers. These opinions we have already seen; and they revolved about a case in which the sacrament could be administered but where it was considered unnecessary for salvation. Calvin, Zwingli, and the Anabaptists were not concerned with a hypothetical case in which a child was beyond the reach of baptism; they were dealing with the experiential situation in which parents found themselves from day to day. The Anabaptists did not baptize; Calvin and Zwingli did but felt no urgency in doing so, for they considered the sacrament unnecessary for the child's salvation. Since these were the men who prompted Trent's discussion in its fifth and sixth sessions, we may fairly conclude that the council too envisioned a case where baptism could be administered, and insisted that here it must be administered.

Newborn Infants

The third factor in the Cajetan decision is closely related to the second; it is the fact that the council spoke of the "newly-born." This is further evidence that they envisioned the Reformers in their decrees. They were discussing children within reach of baptism, not those for whom the sacrament was a very dubious possibility.

Each of these three factors could well account for Trent's cryptic statement that Cajetan's theory "did not pertain to the teaching on baptism." The general necessity of baptism proclaimed by Trent left Cajetan sufficient theological latitude to suggest that not only martyrdom but the faith of the parents might be the instrument of a child's salvation. Moreover, the cardinal was dealing with children who were still in the womb, and so considered beyond reach of baptism both for theological and medical considerations.

Before we can conclude, however, that Cajetan emerged completely unscathed from the deliberations of Trent, there is one final fact to be considered. In its statements on justification the council defined the doctrine that the transferal from original sin to the state of grace was effected by the sacrament of baptism or by its *votum*. Since unbaptized infants are incapable of such a *votum,* many theologians would conclude that they are necessarily lost. Although some of the liberal theologians would concede a problem here but insist on exploring the nature of that *votum,* others would deny that the decree has any relevance at all to the case of an unbaptized infant.

Adopting Paul Horger's detailed analysis of the fifth and sixth sessions of Trent, Santos feels that in its decree on the *votum* of baptism the council was concerned only with the justification of an adult.[12] In opposition to the Protestant position that faith alone justifies, Trent insisted that baptism is also necessary for salvation. The sacrament is not so necessary, however, that without it no one can be saved; and for this reason the conciliar Fathers underscored the existence of a *votum* which could also justify. There is not sufficient evidence, however, says Santos, to warrant our deducing from the Tridentine formula a necessity of means that would put unbaptized infants beyond hope of salvation. The bishops of the council, he notes, were following the lead of Aquinas; and Thomas in his discussion of the *votum* of baptism spoke of the explicit desire of a catechumen for the sacrament; he was concerned, therefore, with an adult who had been duly instructed and had the obligation to receive the sacrament. In Santos' view of the matter, therefore, the teaching of Trent would present no real obstacle to the hypothesis of Cardinal Cajetan. In the words of the bishops themselves: "It does not pertain to the teaching on baptism."

If Cajetan's theory did emerge uncensured from its ordeal at Trent, it is nonetheless a tightly defined and narrowly restricted case, one that can afford limited comfort to the liberal theologians. They must still determine whether the magisterium in its other decisions left them latitude enough to search out a way of saving unbaptized babies.

The Council of Florence and the Necessity of Baptism

The Council of Florence in its Decree for the Jacobites, February 1442, declared that baptism must not be put off for forty or eighty days, as some people were accustomed to do. The reason given by the council was

> "the danger of death, which can often happen, for there is no other remedy available to these [infants] except the sacrament of baptism, which delivers them from the powers of the demon and makes them adopted sons of God."[13]

Two questions must be answered in evaluating a statement of this sort: What is its exact meaning? What is its precise dogmatic weight? Although we have here a text taken from an ecumenical council duly approved by Pope Eugene IV, the statement itself is not part of a dogmatic definition, but rather accessory to it; and since the statement was not endorsed by the highest degree of the Church's teaching authority, it is not infallible.

Charles Journet, one of the "conservative" theologians, agrees that Florence's declaration is not a dogmatic definition, but concludes that it certainly has a high degree of doctrinal value. It pertains, he says, to "Catholic teaching" perhaps in the sense that the Church teaches here something already defined in the Council of Carthage.[14] Bernard Leeming believes that the council intended to affirm the doctrine expressed by St. Thomas, which was unquestionably the common doctrine at the time. Leeming, however, does not specify the precise dogmatic value of this affirmation.[15]

Prescinding for the moment from its dogmatic value, we may look more carefully at the text itself and the situation that occasioned it. The postponement of baptism has been a perennial problem in the Church's history. Chrysostom and Nazianzus spoke out against it in the fourth century and Florence felt compelled to do so a thousand years later. Although the motives for postponing the sacrament varied from century to century, the case remained essentially the same: baptism was not being administered at a time when a person could and should receive it. The bishops of Florence rebuked those who failed to baptize an infant when they might have done so. Quite clearly, then, the Council of Florence was concerned with a pastoral situation, not with a hypothetical case in which the sacrament could not be administered.

It is true nevertheless that the council states a general principle in support of its position: there is no other remedy save baptism. Apropos of this we might note, as one theologian does, that this statement admits of another translation: "there is no other remedy available to us by which we can come to their rescue." Even accepting the first translation as correct, we must still say that the principle affirms only a general necessity of baptism. If the statement were absolute, unqualified, it would be incorrect, for it would rule out baptism of blood as a possible agent of salvation for infants, and this the council could not have done.

Whatever dogmatic value we assign to this statement of 1442, therefore, we cannot say that it closes the door to speculation on the possible salvation of unbaptized infants. The words of the council were prompted by pastoral considerations; it was urging the administration of baptism—something that presumes administration is possible. The reason it gave was the general necessity of the sacrament of baptism.

Other Statements from the Magisterium

In his comments on the Council of Florence, Journet says that the bishops may simply have been teaching what had already been defined in the Council of Carthage in 418.[16] This fifth-century council declared quite clearly that "without baptism they cannot enter the kingdom of heaven which is eternal life." Although Carthage was a provincial council, says Journet, its decrees were approved by Pope Zozimus, who thus gave it the force of an ecumenical council. Journet's opinion is based ultimately on a somewhat vague statement of Augustine and is not generally accepted by historians.[17] We must therefore regard Carthage as only one of a series of authoritative statements by the magisterium on the necessity of baptism.

St. Leo the Great in his letter to the bishops of Sicily explained that baptism was usually conferred at Easter and Pentecost but added that in danger of death, it must be conferred at any time, since no one must be denied this "singular remedy."[18]

A letter attributed to Pope Siricius was later sent to Pepin and Charlemagne to indicate the practice of the Church. This letter implied that anyone "who died without the sacred font would lose both the Kingdom and eternal life."[19]

In the eighth century Pope Gregory II made more explicit the directives of Leo the Great. Baptism, he said, must be administered at Easter and Pentecost. In cases where there was a danger of death, however, the sacrament was to be administered at once "lest [souls] perish in eternity."[20]

The popes and bishops whose statements we have just read were obviously proclaiming not only Christ's command to baptize but the reason that prompted it. According to the command of Christ every man must be baptized, for "unless a man be born again of water and the Spirit he cannot enter into the kingdom of God" (John 3:5). Baptism is necessary, therefore, with a necessity of means, but no theologian or exegete would conclude from these texts to an absolute necessity of the sacrament. To do more would be to rule out martyrdom and baptism of desire as channels of grace. In the texts we have just read, the Church's magisterium repeats the command of Christ much as Christ gave it without the theological distinctions that flow from the total context of his teaching. In the pastoral situation that prompted her words, it is difficult to see how she would have spoken otherwise.

The Allocution of Pius XII
to the Italian Midwives

Quite another matter is the Allocution of Pope Pius XII to the convention of Italian midwives:

> "All that we have said about the protection and care
> of natural life is with even greater reason true of the

supernatural life, which the newborn child receives with baptism. In the present dispensation there is no other means of communicating this life to the child, who has not yet the use of reason. And yet the state of grace is absolutely necessary for salvation: without it supernatural happiness, the beatific vision of God, cannot be attained. In an adult an act of love may suffice to obtain him sanctifying grace and so supply for the lack of baptism; to the child still unborn, or newly born, this way is not open. If therefore we remember that charity towards our neighbor obliges us to assist him in case of necessity; that this obligation is the graver and more urgent according to the greatness of the good to be procured or the evil to be avoided, and according to the inability of the needy one to help himself; then it is easy to understand the importance of providing for the baptism of a child, devoid of the use of reason and in grave danger or even certainty of death."[21]

A papal allocution is not the ordinary vehicle for an infallible pronouncement, and nothing in the context of his talk indicates that the pope is making an *ex cathedra* statement. Nevertheless, such allocutions are part of the ordinary teaching of the Holy Father and as such they command our attention.[22] The impact of the pope's address upon our own question was immediate and obvious. No theologian may make the bald assertion that infants are saved by baptism of desire or by any other substitute for the sacrament. On the other hand we need not conclude that the door has been closed on all discussion of infant salvation.

It is true that the Spanish theologians Lopez Martinez and

Espeja feel that the pope terminated the present controversy by embracing the conservative position.[23] Other observers, however, even in the conservative camp, disagree with their Spanish colleagues. A. Minon thinks that the pope is taking a disciplinary stand in a practical matter, confirming but not imposing the conservative position.[24] Van Roo, Fernandez and Renwart do not believe that the question has been definitively and irrevocably closed.[25]

Such divergent theological reaction to the pope's statement would lead us to conclude, therefore, that the discussion of infant salvation has not been officially terminated. A closer look at the pope's allocution will indicate more clearly why this is so.

In speaking to the midwives the pope made three statements that bear directly on our problem:

1. In the present dispensation, there is no means other than the sacrament of baptism of communicating sanctifying grace to a child who has not attained the use of reason.

2. In an adult an act of love may supply for the lack of baptism.

3. This way is not open to a child still unborn or newly born.

The first statement is, it seems, broader than the Holy Father intended it to be. He certainly had no intention of ruling out martyrdom as a possible means of salvation for the unbaptized child. The liberal theologian might ask, therefore, whether he intended to rule out every possible substitute for infant baptism?

The second statement touches on the essential notion in the idea of baptism of desire. "If any man love me . . . my Father will love him, and we will come to him and make our abode with him" (John 14:23). Implicit in this act of love, of course, is a desire for the sacrament of baptism. This is the traditional idea of baptism of desire as it is found in the teaching of the Church and of theologians over the centuries. Liberal theologians have asked, however, whether this is the only interpretation that can be put upon the idea. As we have seen, they have investigated the possibility of broadening the idea to include a desire made by the child's parents, even by the Church itself.

In a somewhat different vein Angel Santos has observed that the Holy Father was addressing a group of Catholic midwives. His remarks, therefore, are not easily extended to a non-Christian country where there could be no question of a child's baptism.[26]

We might also note that the pope, since he urged the administration of the sacrament, was considering a case where its administration was possible. The liberal theologian might ask whether he intended his observations to apply to a case in which the sacrament simply could not be conferred.

Entirely apart from the dogmatic value of the pope's allocution, therefore, the number of problems that surround the interpretation of his remarks would lead us to conclude with Renwart, Fernandez, and Van Roo that the question has not been definitively and irrevocably closed.

The crucial problem, of course, is that of the dogmatic value of the statement that baptism of desire—an act of love—is not accessible to children. This certainly is the traditional view of the Fathers and theologians through the centuries. The question remains: Is that impossibility of baptism of desire a revealed truth? Or is it a philosophical truth necessary to safeguard revealed truth? Or is it merely a conclusion by human reason from premises that admit of further investigation? The pope does not indicate the answer to these questions. In the light of the other problems that surround his allocution it would seem that they can be answered only by a massive re-evaluation of the notion of baptism of desire as it is found in the teaching of the Fathers and theologians over the centuries.

Magisterium: Summary and Conclusions

From the Council of Carthage in the fifth century to the Allocution of Pius XII in our own day the Church's decrees on the necessity of baptism have been motivated by her pastoral concern for the salvation of souls. The question of baptism affected the practice of the Church, and in this it differed from other questions, such as that of fire in purgatory or relations in the Trinity. When the Church spoke out on the problem, therefore, she did so to urge her people to baptize their children or to be baptized themselves. Since her aims were primarily practical rather than pedagogical, she would have served no pastoral purpose in urging her people to the impossible or even in discussing a case where baptism was out of the question. Hence we may fairly conclude that her injunctions, and the reasoning with which she argued them, were concerned with cases in which baptism was possible. A second important conclusion would be that the Church has officially been silent on the question of an infant whose baptism is physically or morally impossible.

In discussing cases where baptism is possible the Church has indeed appealed to a general principle—the necessity of baptism. But until modern times she contented herself with defining this as a general necessity of means, and refrained from mentioning the extraordinary cases always admitted in the Church—martyrdom and baptism of desire. While the Allocution of Pius XII imposed certain restrictions on theologians, it did leave them room to speculate. While they may not flatly assert that baptism of desire is possible for infants, they are free to speculate about the possibility, to advance theories and hypotheses with normal scientific caution. Moreover, they would seem to be at liberty to discuss the problem of an infant whose baptism is simply out of the question. Since the Holy Father was urging the administration of baptism, he was obviously addressing himself to a case in which its administration was possible. Theologians therefore are quite free to consider a case where administration of the sacrament is impossible. While they may not say that all infants are saved or that all are given an opportunity to choose God, they are free to investigate the context of tradition; they are free to question the dogmatic value of the documents on which the common opinion of theologians is based; they are at liberty to seek an ever more precise understanding of such ideas as baptism of desire and of blood, the salvific will of God, the existence of limbo.

While theologians are free to turn back to the sources of faith in search of greater precision, deeper understanding, it may be asked whether they can find anything to offer them hope. Perhaps tradition stands so firmly against a "liberal solution" that the freedom to investigate will lead the liberal theologians to the conservative camp. The conservatives believe this to be so.

THE NECESSITY OF BAPTISM: B—THE FATHERS OF THE CHURCH

Bernard Leeming concludes his brief study of the first seven centuries of patristic thought with the words:

"The Church, as far as all evidence shows, from the
second to the seventh century universally believed it
to be revealed that an infant dying before any use of
reason, and unbaptized, cannot attain to the beatific
vision."[27]

Charles Journet, quite in sympathy with Leeming, is more
cautious in his appraisal of the same period:

"The Church as it passed through the centuries . . .
has left us some traces, by nature inadequate, of its
baptismal faith. We see her careful to baptize infants because of her apostolic mission. She believes
that she purifies them of a stain of sin not committed
but contracted at birth. Thus she saves them from
perdition."[28]

William Van Roo, S.J., no enthusiast of the liberal cause, is
still more reserved in his judgment of these years. Augustine,
he says, was personally convinced that infants are not saved
and testifies that this is the faith of the Church. In Van Roo's
opinion Augustine's conviction sets the problem but does not
settle it. Even though it can be shown, he continues, that this
is a conviction that goes back to Cyprian and Tertullian and is
found in East and West prior to Pelagianism, it does not settle the question concerning the force of this teaching:

"Do these texts give us an answer to *our* question?
What questions were they answering? And even if
the formulation of the problem materially is the
same, what were the terms of the problem as they
understood it? Even if these Fathers regarded it as

of faith that children dying without baptism are not saved, one must determine the alternate to which they were opposed. . . . It is important to recognize that in all human testimony there is a formal sense which must be determined from the full historical context. We must determine that sense, not simply assume that it is the same as ours."[29]

THE NECESSITY OF BAPTISM: C—THE SCHOLASTIC THEOLOGIANS

The scholastic theologians of the Middle Ages offer no encouragement to liberal theories. As we have seen, scholastic theology was acquainted with "salvation theories." One of these theories concerned the case of a child dying on the way to baptism; another revolved about the priest's lack of intention in administering baptism. Dr. Landgraf, the distinguished medievalist, mentions another still more general theory of salvation when baptism was inculpably beyond reach.[30] A number of the great scholastics were ready to concede a point to these cases, but by way of privileged exception. The possibility of such privilege being a normal way of salvation was quite opposed to their thinking.

The opinions of the medieval theologians, however, are not an insurmountable obstacle to liberal speculations. The doctrine of limbo, a common opinion of medieval theology, was effectively challenged in the seventeenth and eighteenth centuries. The liberal theologians hope to issue an equally successful challenge to medieval thought on the possible salvation of an unbaptized infant.

They would ask the same questions of the Scholastics that Van Roo put to the Fathers of the Church. Do these men give us an answer to *our* problem? What were the terms of the problem as they understood it? There has been a general development of theology over these intervening centuries. The problem as we have it today, therefore, is being stated in terms that would have been unfamiliar, to say the least, to the men of the Middle Ages; one thinks, for example, of the "unconscious desire of membership" in the Church. Then too, medieval thought was conditioned by its limited geographical and political horizons. For these men Europe was very nearly the world; the dramatic discoveries of the fifteenth and sixteenth centuries lay far beyond the age of the Scholastics. The problems posed by entire continents where the gospel was completely unknown did not play an important part in their thinking. For practical purposes their horizons were those of Christian Europe; and this limited vision undoubtedly conditioned their views of God's salvific will and the promulgation of the gospel.

THE NECESSITY OF BAPTISM: D— THEOLOGIANS OF OUR DAY

Twenty years ago hardly a theologian might have been cited in favor of a broader view of infant salvation. The picture has changed in the past two decades and it continues to change. A number of respected writers have shown that they are not entirely unsympathetic to some forms of the new development. Among them L. Richard, Glorieux, Schmaus, Beni, Janssens, Pies, Schillebeeckx, Sanders, Minges, Bäuerle, Feuling, Sauras, Fernandez, and perhaps Karl Rahner.[31]

One robin does not make a spring, nor do a dozen theologians constitute a theological revolution. Although they have been impressed by the posture of one or more of the salvation theories, neither these theologians nor any others have yet done the sweeping research necessary to bolster adequately a theory of unbaptized infant salvation. Nevertheless they con-

stitute an array impressive enough to make one hesitate to
declare a common and certain theological opinion the conservative position that infants are necessarily lost if they die
unbaptized.

THE FATE OF INFANTS DYING IN ORIGINAL SIN

There are in the records of the Church numerous documents that speak of children dying in the state of original sin.
Now the very possibility of anyone's dying in the state of
original sin is a challenge to some of the liberal theories. It
poses a problem for Boudes, who holds that all unbaptized
infants could be saved by the *votum ecclesiae.* The idea is
equally awkward for those who say that unbaptized children
may be offered a choice as a result of which they could go
either to heaven or to hell. Beyond doubt, then, these documents—there are four of them—seem to imperil at least some
of the salvation theories.

Pope Innocent III in his famous letter to the Archbishop
of Arles, *Maiores ecclesiae causae,* writes:

> "The punishment of original sin is the privation of
> the vision of God; the punishment of actual sin is
> the torment of eternal fire."[32]

Even more explicit is the profession of faith sent Michael
Palaeologus by Clement IV and later incorporated into the
Acts of the Second Council of Lyons:

> "The souls of those who die in mortal or in original
> sin alone descend immediately to hell to be punished,
> however, with unequal punishments."[33]

Pope John XXII used the same words in his epistle to the Armenians except that he added that such souls

> "would be punished with different penalties and in different places."[34]

And finally the Council of Florence with its decree for the Greeks repeated the formula of the Second Council of Lyons, omitting the "and in different places" of John XXII.

From these four documents theologians conclude with all certitude that those who die in original sin are forever deprived of the beatific vision. Must they also conclude that some people do as a matter of fact die with only original sin on their souls?

These documents find their most authoritative statement in the Council of Florence. Since we are dealing with a dogmatic definition, it is most important to determine precisely what Florence intended to define. At this council the Latin and Greek bishops were of differing views about the time at which the particular judgment took place.[35] Florence addressed itself precisely to this problem and consequently in its definition laid all emphasis on the word "immediately":

> "the souls of those who die in actual mortal sin, or only in original sin go immediately (*mox*) down to hell, to be punished, however, with different penalties."[36]

The council intended to lay to rest the idea that retribution for sin is delayed in the next life until the resurrection of the body. Since the immediacy of the sanction, therefore, is the object of its definition, the council did not define that there are as a matter of fact souls who die in mortal sin or original sin alone.

The proposition, however, does have a certain dogmatic value, which still must be determined.

"The definition," says Leeming, "certainly takes for granted the possibility of there being such souls [who die in original sin]; and if there is a possibility of one soul dying in original sin, it is not easy to see why there should not be many."[37]

Some of the liberal theologians, however, are unwilling to admit the fact of anyone dying in original sin, and so they treat as hypothetical the phrase "those who die . . . only in original sin." They would interpret Florence in this way: "*If* any die in original sin, and we do not know if there are such. . . ." Fernandez, who is sympathetic to the liberal position, and Leeming, who is not, both reject this interpretation. "Evasive, a subterfuge," says Fernandez. "Certainly appears somewhat arbitrary," writes the English Leeming.[38]

According to another interpretation the council simply made use of current theological categories in speaking of those dying in actual sin or in original sin alone. Van Roo finds this no more persuasive than the first interpretation.[39] The question of the fate of unbaptized infants, he says, was in the air at the time; it occasioned a letter of Benedict XII to the Armenians a century earlier (1341) giving a list of errors which some said were current among the Armenians. The sixth of these errors is that the souls of unbaptized infants go after death to a kind of terrestrial paradise, but if the parents are not Christian, the souls of their unbaptized infants join the parents in the other world, wherever the parents may be. Since these same Armenian bishops met the following year to deny that the error was theirs, one may wonder whether this century-old question, closed apparently by the Armenian Church, was still an issue at the time of the Council of Florence, as Van Roo says. Whether it was or not, the decree of Florence does seem to suggest more than the liberals are willing to concede.

At least one liberal theologian, Peter Gumpel, S.J., sees no difficulty in admitting Leeming's interpretation of Florence. It is perfectly true, he says, that the definition takes for granted the possibility of there being souls who die with only original sin. And this is a serious argument against those who say that it would be impossible for there to be such souls in the present order of providence. One may even go further, he adds, and take for granted the reality of there being such souls. But it is not clear, he concludes, that the formula envisions directly every possible category of these infants.[40] As we saw earlier, the problem of the unbaptized child is not one problem but many; for example, children of Jewish, pagan, Christian parents each present quite different problems. Is it clear that Florence was speaking of all of them? Is it historically certain that even ecclesiastical writers of the period would attribute the same degree of theological certainty to the damnation of every possible category?

A still more basic question is that of the dogmatic value of the council's statement. Granted for the moment that it did envision either the possibility or the reality of souls dying with original sin alone, what limitation does this fact put upon our own thinking?

According to one view of the matter, councils, even in the reasoning that accompanies their definition, speak in the name of the Church, express her mind, and must be interpreted with a view to the meaning commonly attached in the Church to the terms and language used. If this view means that the Council of Florence has given us Catholic teaching, a teaching that cannot be gainsaid, then it encounters certain difficulties from parallel situations in the history of dogma.

The Council of Carthage (418), when defining the necessity of baptism, said that infants would fall to the devil's lot.[41] This statement was not the object of a definition, but it did accompany a definition. As we saw in the first chapter, Carthage reflected the rigorous opinions of Augustine during his Pelagian debates. Over the centuries, however, theological opinion has felt free to move away from the pessimistic views of Augustine. This freedom of action would not have existed, it would seem, had the statement of Carthage been truly Catholic teaching. The cases of Carthage and Florence are not perfectly parallel, but they do show the possible problems that could arise from exaggerating the dogmatic value of the reasons or considerations that accompany a conciliar definition.

Van Roo is more cautious in his evaluation of the Florentine document. He prefers to speak of a *sensus ecclesiae,* a conviction or persuasion of the Church, without committing himself to defining the precise theological value of this persuasion.[42]

The hard fact is, it seems, that we are once again in an area of theology that itself calls for investigation. Few terms are as vague or unsatisfactory at present as "the mind of the Church" —the *sensus ecclesiae*. The term and the reality it embraces are themselves subjects of discussion in the theological world. As a result it is an unwieldy tool in debate. And to that extent at least its usefulness as an objection to the liberal theories is weakened.

THE EXISTENCE OF LIMBO

In our earlier chapters we saw something of the "logic of limbo." Its existence is deduced from several propositions strongly defended by conservative theologians:

1. Baptism by blood, water or desire is necessary for salvation after promulgation of the gospel.
2. An infant is incapable of baptism of desire.
3. Hence unbaptized, unmartyred children die in the state of original sin.
4. The punishment of original sin is the loss of the beatific vision, but not the torment of hell.

On these premises theologians of the past have concluded to the existence of limbo. Obviously we are in the presence of a well-reasoned theological conclusion. Is this conclusion anything more than an opinion of theologians? Bishop Gaudel and Abbé Michel, both distinguished theologians, believe that it is. "An orthodox belief" is Gaudel's description of limbo. "It is a virtually revealed truth," said Michel, "a common doctrine from which it would be rash to depart."[43]

In recent years, however, a number of voices have been raised in protest. "Purely a scholastic creation" is the way one of them describes limbo. Limbo, says another, is "only a theological conclusion, capable of modification, even of revision."[44] The objections offered to the classic theory of limbo are numerous, but the one most frequently and forcefully argued is that of the salvific will of God. How can we maintain, the liberal theologians ask, that no one is damned except by his own fault while at the same time we say that a child innocent of any personal sin is excluded from heaven? But the liberals object to limbo on other grounds as well. How, they ask, can we reconcile the notion of a limbo free of pain or regret with the fact that in the present order of things there is but one destiny for man—the vision of God? Do we not thereby cloud to some extent the true conception of the supernatural? There is a curious difference too in the way theologians explain the eternity of hell and the eternity of limbo. Souls remain eternally in hell, it is said, because their wills are unchangeably fixed in evil, eternally incapable of changing their orientation and accepting the grace of pardon, even supposing that God should offer it. On the other hand children remain eternally in limbo even though they present no obstacle to grace should it be offered.

Since we have already discussed limbo at some length, the reader is in a position to draw his own conclusions on the subject. Nevertheless, there is one observation that bears repetition.

Limbo, we must notice, is not a simple idea but a concept compounded of two quite distinct elements; (1) the exclusion of unbaptized infants from heaven; (2) the absence in their case of the torments of hell—the pain of sense and sorrow over their exile. In any discussion of limbo the second factor is the important one, since it is this that distinguishes limbo from hell. Our own investigations led us to conclude that the idea of limbo as a place free of the torments of hell is a safe explanation of a difficult question held by the majority of Catholic theologians. Given the tortured history of the question, it would be difficult to assign to it any greater dogmatic value. The other factor in the idea of limbo—the exclusion of unbaptized infants from heaven—is the theme of the fourth and fifth chapters of our study.

Good theological method demands that we keep these two factors distinct. The fact is, however, that theological writing of the past fifteen years has not always done so, to the confusion of the entire issue. Conservative theologians who offer the existence of limbo as an argument against the salvation theories have in reality begged the question. They assume what they must prove—that unbaptized infants are indeed excluded from heaven.

THE SALVIFIC WILL OF GOD

Limbo stands on the two dogmatic pillars of original sin and the necessity of baptism. Adam sinned and left to his descendants a legacy of exile. When Christ came to remedy the tragedy, he channeled his merits to the human race through the sacrament of baptism. Since four-fifths of the earth's surface is water, he could hardly have devised a simpler means of regeneration. Yet the very prodigality of the Redeemer seemed to place a great part of the race beyond redemption. In the present economy of salvation baptism is not only a means of regeneration but a necessary means; and without it infants, say the traditional theologians, are forever beyond the pale of salvation. However closely reasoned this conclusion might be, it seemed to many to run contrary to a fundamental fact of revelation—the salvific will of God.

> "I will put enmity between you and the woman, between your seed and her seed; he shall crush your head, and you shall lie in wait for his heel." (Gen. 3:15)

Here we have the first evidence of God's desire to rebuild what man had destroyed. It is the first scriptural evidence of what men would later call God's salvific will—his sincere desire to save the souls of men. The notion is a complex one, and many have run aground in their attempts to understand it.

The Calvinists, for instance, believed that even before Adam had sinned, God's plans called for a hell to which some men were destined. God impelled these men to sin even as he moved the predestined to virtue. Cornelius Jansenius had a somewhat different view, but it was scarcely less pessimistic.

God's original plan had not included a division of the human race into the elect and the damned. When Adam sinned, however, the human race became a *massa damnata*. God chose to leave certain men in this state. For them Christ neither suffered nor died. Since they have no grace from Christ to win their salvation, they must remain among the damned. And among this group of the damned Jansenius numbered the children who died without baptism.

The Bible, of course, tells quite a different story of God's salvific will. When God promised mankind a redeemer, he placed no qualifications on his promise. In setting aside for himself a chosen people he did not reject the Gentiles. To the contrary, he promised Abraham: "In your descendants all the nations of the earth shall be blessed" (Gen. 22:18).

St. Paul clearly proclaimed this universal character of God's salvific will:

> "I urge therefore, first of all, that supplications, prayers, intercessions and thanksgivings be made for all men; for kings, and for all in high positions, that we may lead a quiet and peaceful life in all piety and worthy behavior. This is good and agreeable in the sight of God our Saviour, *who wishes all men to be saved and to come to the knowledge of the truth.* For there is one God, and one Mediator between God and men, himself man, Christ Jesus, *who gave himself a ransom for all,* bearing witness in his own time." (1 Tim. 2:1-6)

In this text St. Paul sets in clear relief the sincerity of God's desire to save all men. God's desire is without limit, for it embraces "all men"; his sincerity is beyond question because he sent "Christ who gave himself a ransom for all."

St. Peter too preached the universality of God's call to salvation. In his second epistle he states:

> "The Lord does not delay in his promises, but for your sake is long-suffering, not wishing that any should perish, but that all should turn to repentance." (2 Peter 3:9)

St. John is a faithful reflection of the ideas of Peter and Paul. The Word is the true light that "enlightens every man who comes into the world" (John 1:9). Jesus is the lamb who "takes away the sin of the world" (John 1:29). In his first epistle he writes:

> "But if anyone sins, we have an advocate with the Father, Jesus Christ the just; and he is a propitiation for our sins, not for ours only, but for those of the whole world." (1 John 2: 1-2).

However forcefully the Bible teaches the sincerity of God's will to save each man, a problem remains; there is evidence that not all men will be saved. In his description of the last judgment Christ speaks of those who will depart from him under an eternal curse. St. Paul enumerates the categories of sinners who will not possess the kingdom of God. If God's desire to save these men is sincere, why are they not saved? As we have seen, St. Peter placed the blame on the shoulders of men (2 Peter 3:9). As Peter indicates, it is God's wish that all repent; yet some refuse to do penance in spite of the ransom that Christ paid for their salvation.

Two facts, therefore, about the nature of God's salvific will emerge from Scripture. God's desire to save men is sincere but it is not absolute, it does not override the free will of men. God sincerely desires their repentance, but they must repent.

Putting it another way, we would say that God's salvific will was conditioned; once this condition has been fulfilled, the conditioned will becomes absolute. If the condition is not fulfilled, the salvific will ceases to be operative. What is the condition? According to a current opinion among theologians, it is God's prevision of the person dying in the state of grace.

In general this same condition applies to infants as well as to adults. In their case, however, a peculiar difficulty arises; the possible lack of grace cannot be attributed in any way to an infant's abuse of its free will. In their attempts to solve this problem theologians have tried to link in some way the absence of grace to a human will; in this case it will be the will of the adult who is responsible for the child. With this in mind theologians try to determine more accurately the point at which God's salvific will either becomes absolute or ceases to be operative. In doing so they normally speak of two distinct situations; in one of these the child dies unbaptized because of the negligence of some adult; in the other the adult is blameless.

In the first case God wills the salvation of the infant on the condition that adults correctly make use of their free wills. If they do so, the child will be baptized and die in the state of grace. If they fail to do so, God's salvific will ceases and the child dies unregenerated. In this case God has been faithful to his own salvific will, since he has confided the supernatural well-being of these children to adults as he has their nourishment and education. Moreover, he does much by his grace to encourage the adults to baptize a child.

Theologians face a far more difficult problem, however, when they consider the case of a child whose baptism is physically impossible. An expectant mother, let us say, is struck and killed by an automobile while shopping. Here the physical causes inducing death concur with a series of adult actions to prevent the administration of baptism. When God foresees the conjunction of these two forces, his salvific will ceases to be operative. According to theologians, however, his salvific will remains intact for two reasons. First, he is not obliged to interfere with the normal play of secondary causes, even though these would put the child beyond the reach of baptism. Secondly, he has provided a means for the child's salvation by the institution of baptism.

This solution to the problem seems to some to be no solution at all. Can we sincerely say, asks one, that God gave these infants a means of salvation when they died without the possibility of receiving the baptism which is so necessary to their salvation?[45] These men find it difficult to believe that Christ, in instituting the sacrament of baptism, intended thereby to set the greater part of mankind beyond the pale of his redemptive influence.[46] It would be simpler, some of them think, to opt for the solution of Vasquez, who denied that God's salvific will extended to infants.[47]

"Do we not actually renounce the salvific will of God, by contenting ourselves with such [an explanation]?" Is God's will truly salvific for a child whom it fails to reach even though unopposed by the child? Is the sacrament of baptism truly a sufficient help to salvation when it is not personally, really available to him? The questions are asked by Charles Journet.[48] Some, he continues, try to avoid this challenge to God's salvific will by granting to infants the possibility of baptism of desire. Journet suggests a re-evaluation of God's salvific will.

The error that both the liberals and the conservatives share in the matter of infant salvation, he says, is that they think only in terms of supernatural salvation.

The truth to be safeguarded, says Journet, is that Christ's salvific will extends to every infant, but it is operative in two distinctly different ways. To some he gives the salvation which is due their nature, climaxing it with a life of happiness. To others he gives a more marvellous salvation, due in no way to their nature, which introduces them to the world of true beatitude.

Journet's Theory of God's Salvific Will[49]

The universality of Christ's redemptive work, says Journet, does not imply that God confers the same gifts on all. But if his gifts are unequal, God nevertheless refuses to no one what is due his nature. If we ask, therefore, whether every child, even the unbaptized, profits by the redemptive work of Christ, the answer is that Christ refuses to no infant what is due it; in many cases he gives them infinitely more than is their due.

At two successive moments Christ confers on unbaptized children gifts that are due their natures. At the instant of their death he gives them a definitive victory over concupiscence by transferring them to a world of happiness. At the end of time he gives them a final victory over death by seeing to their resurrection. Thus it is to Christ that these children owe their restitution to the physical and moral fullness of their human natures. Each of these ideas warrants some explanation.

It is one of the paradoxes of our human condition, says Journet, that the resurrection of our bodies appears to be demanded by our nature even though it can be effected only by a miracle. It is axiomatic to Thomistic philosophy that nothing contrary to nature can perdure. The immortality of the soul, therefore, would seem to demand the resurrection of the body, for the union of the two is natural. Nonetheless we know through revelation that our triumph over death is due to the miraculous power of Christ. The effects of this power, however, are not identical in all. Although all will rise from the dead at the end of time, only the just will find their resurrection modeled on the glorious resurrection of Christ.

The other "natural" triumph of infants that is due to the good offices of Christ is their victory over the moral disorder of concupiscence. And this is theirs immediately at their death when they are transferred to the world of limbo. The victory can be considered a natural one because it sets right the order of nature. Because of original sin man is unable to love God above all things, nor can he obey all the precepts of the natural law. Mankind has lost the spontaneous élan by which it tends to the good that is proportioned to its nature, but it has not lost this proportion itself; man's natural end remains. We must notice, therefore, that a child who is born in original sin is enfeebled only in relation to our universe of fallen and redeemed human nature. And although his human powers are not up to the totality of the human task that confronts him, he retains the integrity and basic equilibrium of his nature. In the world of limbo, moreover, the disparity between task and resources is not present. The child is not only stabilized eternally in the integrity of his nature, but he deploys spontaneously the activities of knowledge and love which are proper to a separated soul. He knows in a manner which is native to the angels, becoming first of all totally transparent to himself and then aware of the world about him. At the final resurrection he will find his happiness in exercising a full vigorous activity of knowledge and love. And this happiness he will owe to Christ. For it is from Christ that he has received the full natural life of the body as well as that of the soul.

In Journet's theory, therefore, unbaptized infants are embraced by the salvific will of God. Christ took human nature in order to rehabilitate it; and it is to him that these children owe their happiness in limbo; it is to him that they will owe the resurrection of their bodies, no longer feeble and fragile but fully adapted to a life of knowledge and love.

These children are gathered about Christ, says Journet, and conformed to him so far as he has become the head and the healer of mankind. But they are separated from him so far as he is the prince of the new universe of grace and glory. They know the circumstances of the redemption that concern the reestablishment of human nature, but they are unaware of the circumstances which concern the regeneration of the human race, adoptive filiation and the beatific vision. The natural love they have of God inaugurates between them and God a natural friendship.

In Journet's opinion they could surmise the existence of a world superior to their own from which would arrive messages and illuminations. They will even catch glimpses of Christ at times without, however, divining his full mystery . . . And they will desire with a natural desire to see God directly, knowing at the same time that such a desire is aimed at a goal that is beyond their powers and superior to their destiny.

Journet therefore concludes that the death of an unbaptized infant is not a miscarriage but a flowering of providence. It inaugurates the moment in which God's salvific will for them is fulfilled, the will to restore the fullness of their human nature; and it is this that gives eternal meaning to their brief sojourn on earth.

Journet's theory is similar in many respects to that proposed by Suarez in the sixteenth century; and to some extent it has met criticisms similar to those levelled against the Jesuit theologian. Suarez's liberal views, it was once said, imperiled the supernatural order. In recent months Journet's theory has been criticized as "one of the most dangerous of the deviations among Catholics who are writing on the problem of infant salvation."[50] Journet, it is charged, has not resolved the problem of God's salvific will but has instead denied one of the premises to the problem, i.e. that God wills the supernatural salvation of every man. According to this criticism, therefore, Journet has in effect removed a vast number of men from the influence of God's true salvific will.

BAPTISM OF DESIRE

So many of the salvation theories revolve about some form of baptism of desire that the notion of the *votum baptismi* has become one of the pivotal points in the question of infant salvation. In view of Michel's accusation that the liberal theologians have not always clearly distinguished between baptism of desire and the desire of baptism, some clarification of these ideas is imperative.[51]

When Trent defined the proposition that the process of justification is effected by baptism or its *votum,* it was canonizing a very ancient idea. Augustine wrote that "not only suffering for Christ could supply for the lack of baptism but also faith and a conversion of the heart."[52] And when Valentinian II was killed while still a catechumen, Ambrose was sure that he had received the grace of justification. "[The emperor] made known to me his desire . . . that I initiate and baptize him. Does he not, therefore, have the grace which he desired . . . Certainly he received it because he requested it."[53] Pope Innocent II appealed to the doctrine of Ambrose and Augustine when he declared that a man who died unbaptized was saved if he died in the faith confessing the name of Christ.[54] Innocent III said the same of a Jewish convert who died without the sacrament; he would go to heaven, said the pope, not because of the sacrament of faith but because of faith in the sacrament.[55] The medieval theologians refined the notion of the *votum baptismi* by distinguishing between a desire for the sacrament that was animated by charity and one that was not.[56] The latter, they taught, was not an adequate substitute for the sacrament; and it was in this sense that Trent defined the proposition that a desire of the sacrament without perfect charity would not justify a sinner.[57] The power of charity and the necessity of baptism form the theological substructure of the *votum baptismi*. One who loves God above all things is obviously ready to obey the divine command to be reborn of water. His desire need not be vocalized; it need not even be conscious, but could consist in an habitual readiness to do whatever God commands.

Since acts of faith, love and desire are seemingly beyond the powers of an infant, theologians have almost unanimously limited baptism of desire to an adult. An infant, they concluded, is simply incapable of the *votum baptismi*. This traditional posture is corroborated not only by the weight of theological opinion through the centuries but by a conviction that seems to exist in the documents of the Church. Some of these we have already seen: those of Florence, the Roman Catechism, the Allocution of Pius XII to the Italian Midwives. One other statement by the provincial Council of Cologne deserves mention:

> "Faith teaches us that infants, since they are not capable of this desire, are excluded from the kingdom of heaven if they die [unbaptized]."[58]

The conviction does exist, therefore, both among councils and theologians, that infants are incapable of receiving baptism of desire. The problem is to determine whether this conviction is based upon revelation or upon human observation. Is it a revealed truth, Renwart asks, or a conclusion from human and merely debatable premises?[59] To answer that question adequately, the liberal theologian must define the motive that led the Fathers and the councils of the Church to feel that the *votum baptismi* was beyond reach of infants. Until he has done this—and it demands a massive reappraisal of patristic and conciliar thought—his speculations must remain largely hypothetical.

CONCLUSION

The literature of the past three decades allows us few, if any, unchallenged conclusions; nevertheless, the discussion has not been without its value. For one thing, it has brought into focus the many elements of the problem of infant salvation and shown that the weight of tradition does not bear equally on them all. Limbo is perhaps the clearest example of this reappraisal.

The argument had been used against the liberal theologians that the existence of limbo is Catholic teaching; and since unbaptized infants go to limbo, there could be no question of their possible salvation. It now seems quite clear, however, that the idea of limbo is structured on two propositions, one of which has had a troubled history. If a constant theological tradition can be found for the notion that unbaptized infants are excluded from heaven, the same cannot be said of the idea that they are free from the pains of hell. The latter is a more recent thought in the history of Western theology, one that has been vigorously debated, and even in recent times proposed by theologians only with varying degrees of conviction. And while no theologian today would seriously suggest that such infants suffer the torments of hell, the labyrinthine evolution of the idea of limbo precludes its use as an effective argument against the liberal position. If the salvation theories are to be rejected, therefore, it must be done directly, on the evidence offered us by the documents of the Church; and here another clarification has taken place.

The fate of the unbaptized child, it now appears, presents not one problem but many; and the authority of papal and conciliar statements does not touch equally on them all. The death of a child in its mother's womb, for instance, gives pause even to the distinguished theologian Lercher, though he is otherwise firmly established in the conservative camp. The death of a child whose parents are unaware of the law of baptism raises the question of the gospel's promulgation; and while this problem is thorny enough, it lends itself to discussion more readily than an attempt to re-evaluate the law of baptism itself. Only when we come to the newborn child of Catholic parents do we encounter the problem of infant salvation in all its complexity; and even here certain fissures seem to have appeared in the monolithic structure of the conservative stance.

Conservative theologians were once accustomed to mass an imposing array of ecclesiastical documents against the salvation theories. Now it seems that, quite apart from their dogmatic value, these documents are in several categories and of unequal relevance. There are those that speak of baptism in its relation to original sin and justification. And although the necessity of the sacrament is clearly stated here, it seems we could not certainly conclude that it was more than a general necessity. Others urged the administration of baptism, but by that very token they concerned themselves with a situation in which the sacrament could be administered. They were not dealing with the theoretical question of the fate of a child who is completely beyond reach of the sacrament. Finally we encounter those rather recent documents which say that an infant is incapable of baptism of desire. These last are important because they represent a really ancient persuasion in the Church that an infant must receive the sacrament itself if it is to be saved. Both the liberal and the conservative theologians face a challenge here. Until this conviction has been fully evaluated in its historical context, the salvation theories must remain hypotheses. But the conservative theologian can take little comfort in this fact, for he cannot be certain himself whether this persuasion is based on revelation or upon human observation. In either case a vast amount of painstaking research must be done. Perhaps, as one theologian suggests, only the Church can decide the issue. Even if this is true, the Church is unlikely to speak until the evidence has been thoroughly sifted.

The interpretation of the salvific will of God presents theologians of both camps with another formidable task. Perhaps the strongest plank in the liberal platform, it is not a concept that can readily be taken hold of. Pressed too closely by the liberals, it leads easily to a universalist theory of salvation. Unless it is somehow restated by the conservatives, however, it runs the risk of seeming a paradox, especially when confronted by the picture of countless infants beyond any hope of receiving the sacrament. The conservative Journet, as we have seen, feels keenly the inadequacy of the traditional statement of the doctrine of God's salvific will. Nonetheless his reworking of the thesis is disquieting, for it means that a large segment of the human race was never destined for the beatific vision. The idea is not new to the history of theology, but neither is it reassuring. It gives the impression of being an attempt to back away from the problem rather than face it squarely. Less than a third of mankind is Christian; and an impressive part of the non-Christian world dies in infancy. The dimensions of this problem are imposing enough, it seems, to warrant a more positive attempt at solution.

If the discussion of the past thirty years has so far been of value mainly to the theologian, it is not without its pastoral implications. We hardly need the statements of Pius XII and the Holy Office to remind us that salvation theories are highly vulnerable to criticism and could hardly be used to justify delaying the baptism of a child. Anyone who would do so would be seriously lacking in charity and prudence, to say nothing of obedience to the directives of the Church.

The pastoral problem often takes quite a different and more poignant form, however. What are we to say to the anxious questioning of parents who have experienced the unexpected death of an unbaptized infant? On the evidence, limbo is still a safe and widely held answer to the question; as Leeming, for instance, explains it, it is both a beautiful and consoling conception. On the other hand, a mother or father will frequently not be satisfied with the limbo solution however attractively we may state it. Is there any possibility, they will ask, that the child is in heaven? In my opinion the evidence to the contrary is not so clear or compelling that it would force us to deny them all hope of the infant's salvation.

Notes

LIST OF ABBREVIATIONS

DB—Denzinger-Bannwart, *Enchiridion Symbolorum*
DTC—*Dictionnaire de Théologie Catholique*
MC—Mansi, *Sacrorum Conciliorum Nova et Amplissima Collectio*
PG—Migne, *Patrologia Graeca*
PL—Migne, *Patrologia Latina*

CHAPTER I: THE PATRISTIC PERIOD

1. The most ancient reference to the problem of unbaptized children is to be found in the *Apocalypse* of St. Peter, part of the apocryphal literature of the early second century. Written within fifty years of the death of John the Apostle, it consists mainly in visions which picture the beauty of heaven and the ugliness of hell. The author paints in detail the hideous punishments to which sinful men and women are subjected according to their crimes. He pictures a squalid lake in which were buried the women who had given birth to children out of wedlock or who had committed abortion. The children they had hurt were with them, crying, an eternal reproach. "And from them went forth rays of fire and smote the women in the eyes. . . ." Quasten remarks on the importance of the Apocrypha as a clue to the thinking of early Christians. J. Quasten, *Patrology* (Westminster: Newman, 1950), Vol. I, p. 145.

2. His appearance also furnished ample material for the jibes of Orosius and the more accomplished pen of Jerome: "This immense Goliath is filled too with pride; swollen with fleshy might, confident that all is within his power [he is] wholly clothed in air—head, hands and whole body." Paul Orosius, *Liber Apologeticus, PL* 31, c. 1176. "Most doltish

man stuffed with Scottish pudding." Jerome, *Comm. in Ieremiam Prophetam, Prologus, PL* 24, c. 682.

Souter noted that Augustine, Orosius, Marius Mercator, and Prosper spoke of him as British (*Britto, Britannus*), while Jerome appeared to think of him as Irish (*Scottus*). Alexander Souter, *Pelagius' Expositions of Thirteen Epistles of St. Paul* (*Texts and Studies*) (Cambridge: The University Press, 1922-1931). (This edition is the one cited in our references to Pelagius' *Expositiones XIII Epistolarum Pauli.*) Cf. Vol. I, pp. 2 ff. Plinval believes that Pelagius' father may have been of Mediterranean origin; an official, perhaps a doctor, he settled in the Roman province of Britiania and married a woman of the region. *Pélage, son ecrits, sa vie et sa réforme: étude d'histoire littéraire et religieuse* (Paris: Payot, 1943), p. 61.

3. Cf. G. de Plinval, "Les Luttes Pélagiennes": *Histoire de L'Eglise depuis les Origenes, jusqu'à Nos Jours,* publiée sous la direction de Augustin Fliche et Victor Martin (Paris: Bloud and Gay, 1937), Vol. IV, p. 80; also Franz Klasen, *Die innere Entwicklung des Pelagianismus* (Freiburg im Breisgau: Herder, 1882), p. 4.

4. Augustine, *De Natura et Gratia,* 1, *PL* 44, c. 247: ". . . and I saw a man on fire with a burning zeal against those who should in their sins blame the human will and instead, blaming the nature of men, try to find excuse for themselves in this." *Ibid.,* 82: ". . . he spurs on and inflames to a righteous life with Christian exhortations souls grown cold and sluggish."

5. Cf. Klasen, *op. cit.,* p. 13; de Plinval, *Pélage,* p. 234; R. Hedde and E. Aman, "Pélagianisme," *DTC* XII, c. 683; J. Tixeront, *History of Dogmas,* trans. by H. L. B. (St. Louis: Herder, 1923), Vol. II, pp. 433-434; F. Cayré, *Manual of Patrology and History of Theology,* trans. by H. Howitt (Paris: Desclée, 1936), Vol. I, p. 391; E. Portalié, "Augustin," *DTC* I, c. 2381. There is not complete unanimity on this point, however; Wörter has outlined the various opinions that have been defended through the years. Jansenius and Garnier thought the keystone of the Pelagian system to be its insistence that death was natural and not the punishment of sin. Wiggers considered the Pelagian view of infant baptism to be at the basis of their teaching. Julius Müller believed that their superficial idea of sin was the key to Pelagian thought. Cf. Friedrich Wörter, *Der Pelagianismus nach seinen Ursprung und seiner Lehre* (Freiburg im Breisgau, 1886), p. 210. We will make no attempt in this brief sketch of ours to trace the antecedents of the Pelagian doctrine, since this would take us far beyond the scope of our chapter. It will be sufficient to note the various opinions that have been held down through the centuries; Franz Klasen has indicated them briefly. Jerome thought that the Pelagian doctrine was a blend of the teachings of Pythagoras and Mani, Priscillian, Jovinian, and the Euchites. Marius Mercator said that it sprang from the doctrine of Theodore of Mopsuestia, brought to Rome by Rufinus of Syria in 399. Certain English

authors of more recent times would trace Pelagianism to the Druidism of early Britain; Schleiermacher sought its origins in Monasticism. Wörter gave as its explanation the anthropology of the Greek Fathers of the fourth and fifth centuries whose doctrine developed in the struggle against Gnosticism, Fatalism, and Manichaeism. Cf. Klasen, *op. cit.*, pp. 1-4; Wörter, *op. cit.*, pp. 1-208; de Plinval, *Pélage*, pp. 72-121. In our discussion we will restrict ourselves to the writings of Pelagius which are undisputed: *Expositiones xiii epistolarum Pauli* and *Epistola ad Demetriadem*. G. de Plinval has in his very thorough studies extended Pelagius' authorship to many other writings. Since I am in no position to judge the merit of his investigations, I will restrict myself to texts whose authorship is generally agreed upon. M. de Plinval's investigations have thrown light upon one problem in which we are interested, the "eternal life" of the Pelagians. Cf. "Les Luttes Pélagiennes," p. 84, n. 2; *Pélage*, pp. 1-46.

6. Pelagius' *Expositio in Romanos*, V, 12 (Souter, *op. cit.*, p. 45, 1. 11): "by example or pattern." Pelagius, *Ibid.:* "It passed to all who were living in a human [and] not heavenly fashion."

For an excellent analysis of these texts, cf. J. J. Dempsey, *Pelagius' Commentary on St. Paul, a Theological Study* (Rome: Pontificia Universitas, Gregoriana, 1937); also de Plinval, *Pélage*, p. 150 ff.

According to Klasen, Pelagius did not deny original sin until after Celestius had done so openly at Carthage. Cf. Klasen, *op. cit.*, p. 31. From what we have seen of Pelagius' commentary on Romans V, 12, I am inclined to agree with Augustine, who said Pelagius put his own objections in the mouths of others. Augustine, *De Peccatorum Meritis et Remissione*, III, 6, *PL* 44, c. 188. However that may be, there is no doubt that Pelagius openly denied original sin at least after the Council of Diospolis. At that time he clearly stated that Adam's sin hurt only himself; hence a child is born in the state in which Adam was before he sinned; cf. Augustine, *De Peccato Originali*, 14, *PL* 44, c. 392. He described the lot of children at birth as "an unadorned and unpracticed state of goodness." Augustine, *De Gratia Christi*, 34, *PL* 44, c. 376. Cf. Gustave Wiggers, *An Historical Presentation of Augustinism and Pelagianism from the Original Sources*, trans. by R. Emerson Andover (New York, 1840), p. 137; Wörter, *op. cit.*, p. 309; Klasen, *op. cit.*, pp. 13, 31 and 214.

7. Augustine, *Serm.* 294, 1, *PL* 38, c. 1336: " 'Unless one be born again of water and the Holy Spirit, he will not enter the kingdom of God.' If they are not impressed by that idea, they will certainly not think that infants must be baptized. But, they claim, he does not say: 'Unless one be born again of water and the Spirit he will not have salvation or eternal life.' For this [therefore] must children be baptized, that they might also be with Christ in the kingdom of God. They will not be there if they are not baptized. If children, however, die unbaptized they will

have salvation and eternal life, for they are not entangled in any bond of sin."

8. Augustine, *Opus Imperfectum*, I, 53, *PL* 45, c. 1076: "Those whom Christ made good by creation, he makes better by renovation and adoption." Cf. *Ibid.*, VI, 36, c. 1594; *Contra Julianum*, III, 8, *PL* 44, c. 705.

9. *Serm.* 294, 3, 4, *PL* 38, c. 1337: "Behold, I have explained to you what the Kingdom is and what eternal fire is, so that when you profess that a child is not in the Kingdom, you may acknowledge that he is in eternal fire."

10. *De Peccatorum Meritis et Remissione*, I, 26-27, *PL* 44, c. 123; *Ibid.*, I, 34, c. 128; *De Peccato Originali*, 19, *PL* 44, 394.

11. *De Peccatorum Meritis et Remissione*, III, 7, *PL* 44, c. 189: "They could not be damned, however, if they were certainly sinless." Cf. *De Peccato Originali*, 23, *PL* 44, c. 396; *Epist.* 166, 25, *PL* 33, c. 731; *Contra Duas Epistolas Pelagianorum*, I, 49, *PL* 44, c. 570; *De Peccatorum Meritis et Remissione*, I, 23, *PL* 44, c. 122.

12. *Epist.* 186, 27, *PL* 33, c. 826; *De Peccatorum Meritis et Remissione*, I, 40, *PL* 44, c. 132; *Ibid.*, III, 7, c. 189; *Ibid.*, I, 41, c. 132; *Ibid.*, I, 62, c. 145; *Ibid.*, III, 3, c. 187; *De Peccato Originali*, 19, *PL* 44, c. 394; *Ibid.*, 22, c. 395; *Contra Julianum*, VI, 10, *PL* 44, c. 827; *De Peccatorum Meritis et Remissione*, I, 41, *PL* 44, c. 132; *Ibid.*, I, 62, c. 145; *Ibid.*, III, 3, c. 187; *Ibid.*, III, 7, c. 189; *Epist.* 166, 6, *PL* 33, c. 723; *Ibid.*, 25, c. 731; *Ibid.*, 28, c. 733. *De Peccato Originali*, 19, *PL* 44, c. 394; *Ibid.*, 22, c. 395; *Ibid.*, 23, c. 396. *De Nuptiis et Concupiscentia*, II, 32, *PL* 44, c. 455; *Ibid.*, II, 46, c. 463; *Ibid.*, II, 51, c. 466; *Ibid.*, II, 58, c. 471; *De Anima et ejus Origine*, I, 13, *PL* 44, c. 481; *Ibid.*, I, 16, c. 483; *Ibid.*, II, 17, c. 505; *Ibid.*, II, 18, c. 506; *Ibid.*, III, 14, c. 518; *Ibid.*, IV, 16, c. 533; *Contra Duas Epistolas Pelagianorum*, IV, 24, *PL* 44, c. 626; *De Correptione et Gratia*, 12, *PL* 44, c. 923; *De Dono Perseverantiae*, 23, *PL* 45, c. 1006; *Ibid.*, 25, c. 1008; *Ibid.*, 30, c. 1011; *Ibid.*, 31, c. 1012; *Ibid.*, 32, c. 1012; *Serm.* 294, 7, *PL* 38, c. 1339; *Epist.* 157, 11, *PL* 33, c. 678; *Ibid.*, 12, c. 679; *Ibid.*, 19, c. 683; *Epist.* 186, 27, *PL* 33, c. 826; *Ibid.*, 29, c. 827; *Ibid.*, 30, c. 827; *Epist.* 194, 42, *PL* 33, c. 889; *Enchiridion ad Laurentium*, 26, *PL* 40, c. 245; *Ibid.*, 51, c. 256; *Contra Julianum*, III, 25, c. 715; *Ibid.*, IV, 46, c. 761; *Ibid.*, VI, 10, c. 827; *Ibid.*, VI, 52, c. 853; *Ibid.*, VI, 59, c. 858; *Opus Imperfectum*, I, 130, *PL* 45 c. 1130; *Ibid.*, II, 103, c. 1183; *Ibid.*, II, 105, c. 1185; *Ibid.*, II, 135, c. 1198; *Ibid.*, II, 189, c. 1223; *Ibid.*, III, c. 1261; *Contra Julianum*, I, 24, *PL* 44, c. 657; *Ibid.*, II, 9, c. 679; *Ibid.*, III, 8, c. 706; *Ibid.*, III, 9, c. 707; *Ibid.*, IV, 34, c. 756; *Ibid.*, VI, 22, c. 835; *Ibid.*, VI, 31, c. 840; *Ibid.*, VI, 33, c. 841; *Opus Imperfectum*, I, 50, *PL* 45, c. 1073; *Ibid.*, I, 56, c. 1078; *Ibid.*, I, 60, c. 1081; *Ibid.*, I, 64, c. 1084; *Ibid.*, I, 88, c. 1107; *Ibid.*, II, 181, c. 1220; *Ibid.*, III, 99, c. 1289; *Ibid.*, III, 125, c. 1300; *Ibid.*, III, 127, c. 1300; *Ibid.*, III, 137, c. 1302; *Ibid.*, III, 207, c. 1335; *Ibid.*, IV, 77, c. 1383; *Ibid.*, V, 64, c. 1504; *Ibid.*, VI, 20, c. 1546; *De Nuptiis et*

Concupiscentia, I, 1, *PL* 44, c. 413; *Ibid.,* I, 22, c. 426; *Ibid.,* II, 3, c. 438; *Ibid.,* II, 8, c. 441; *Ibid.,* II, 15, c. 445; *Ibid.,* II, 33, c. 455; *Ibid.,* II, 50, c. 465; *Ibid.,* II, 51, c. 467; *Contra Duas Epistolas Pelagianorum,* IV, 24, *PL* 44, c. 626; *De Dono Perseverantiae,* 27, *PL* 45, c. 1009; *Ibid.,* 29, c. 1010; *Epist.* 194, 43, *PL* 33, c. 889; *Ibid.,* 46, c. 890; *De Haeresibus,* 88, *PL* 42, c. 47; *Opus Imperfectum,* III, 199, *PL* 45, c. 1333: "If a child is not wrested from the power of darkness, but remains there, why do you marvel that he is in eternal fire who is not permitted to enter the kingdom of heaven?"; *Serm.* 294, 3, *PL* 38, c. 1337: "He who is not on the right [hand of the Judge] is undoubtedly on the left; therefore, he who [is] not in the kingdom [is] beyond doubt in eternal fire"; *Ibid.,* "Behold, I have explained to you what the kingdom is, and what eternal fire is; so that when you profess that a child is not in the kingdom, you may acknowledge that he is in eternal fire."

13. *Opus Imperfectum,* IV, 122, *PL* 45, c. 1417: To Julian's accusation that Augustine taught "the good and the wicked, i. e. the innocent and the devil, must be tormented by one punishment," Augustine replied, *Ibid.,* c. 1418: "The good and evil are not, as you slanderously say, (to be punished) by one penalty, but we say that the good are [to suffer] no [punishment] while the wicked are to be tormented not by one punishment but by divers punishments for the diversity of their wickedness"; *De Peccatorum Meritis et Remissione,* I, 21, *PL* 44, c. 120; *Contra Julianum,* V, 44, *PL* 44, c. 809: "I do not say, however, that children dying unbaptized are to suffer so great a punishment that it would be better for them not to have been born, since the Lord did not say this of just any sinner but of the most criminal and the most wicked."

14. G. de Plinval, "Les Luttes Pélagiennes," p. 105; Augustine, *Epist.* 177, *PL* 33, c. 764. It was signed by Aurelius, Alpius, Augustine, Evodius, and Possidius.

15. Augustine, *Epist.* 181, 9, *PL* 33, c. 783; *Serm.* 131, 10, *PL* 38, c. 734: "Two communications have been sent to the Apostolic See; whence the rescripts have also come. The matter is closed. . . ."

16. G. de Plinval, "Les Luttes Pélagiennes," p. 107; Marius Mercator, *Commonitorium super Nomine Coelestii,* 4, *PL* 48, c. 75; Pelagius, *Libellus Fidei, PL* 48, c. 488.

17. *MC* IV, c. 350-351.

18. Quesnel, *Dissertationes in Codicem Canonum Ecclesiasticorum,* cap. 13 (ed. Ballerini), *PL* 56, c. 487. The translation follows that of E. Aman, "Milève," *DTC* X, c. 1755-1756. As Aman points out, there has been some question of the authenticity of Canon 3. He believes that the discussion must be considered at an end, for the authenticity of the canon has been solidly established. *Op. cit.,* c. 1754. In agreement with this view are: A. Gaudel, "Péché Originel," *DTC* XII, c. 386; E. Portalié, *op. cit.,* c. 2384; R. Hedde, "Pélagianisme," *DTC* XII, c. 699, Tixeront, *op. cit.,* Vol. II, p. 452, n. 77. A. Gaudel, commenting on the precise import of Canon 3, said that the Council of Carthage envisaged "the

existence of an intermediary state like that the Pelagians dreamed of.
. . . This would imply the temporary entrance of infants into the paradise of the good thief." Cf. "Limbes," *DTC* IX, c. 763. It would seem
that Gaudel is attributing to the Pelagians an idea of Vincentius Victor.
The latter went considerably beyond the Pelagians in his generosity with
unbaptized infants. As Augustine mentions, the Pelagians never dared
promise unbaptized children the kingdom of heaven; Vincentius Victor
admitted children to the kingdom after a temporary sojourn in paradise.
Augustine is quite clear in distinguishing Victor from the Pelagians.
"For he [Vincentius Victor] has accorded to unbaptized infants such
happiness and salvation as even the Pelagian heresy could not have
ventured on doing." *De Origine Animae*, II, 21, *PL* 44, c. 508. "Once
more, if you desire to be a Catholic, do not believe, or say, or teach
that 'some of those persons who have departed this life without Christ's
Baptism, do not in the meantime go into the kingdom of heaven but
into paradise; yet afterwards in the resurrection of the dead, they attain
also to the blessedness of the kingdom of heaven.' Even the Pelagian
heresy was not daring enough to grant them this, although it holds that
infants do not contract original sin." *Ibid.*, III, 19, c. 520. "The new
Pelagian heretics have been most justly condemned by the authority of
Catholic councils and of the Apostolic See, on the ground of their having
dared to give to unbaptized infants a place of rest and salvation, even
apart from the kingdom of heaven. This they would not have dared to
do, if they did not deny their having original sin, and the need of its
remission by the sacrament of baptism. This man, however, [Vincentius
Victor] professes the Catholic belief on this point, admitting that infants are tied in the bonds of original sin, and yet he releases them
from these bonds without the laver of regeneration, and after death,
in his compassion, he introduces them after the resurrection even to
the kingdom of heaven," *Ibid.*, II, 17, c. 505. In his recent book, Abbé
Michel quoted this passage of Bishop Gaudel in full and used it to describe the Pelagian heresy. A. Michel, *Enfants Morts sans Baptême*
(Paris: Téqui, 1954), p. 12 and p. 35. It does not seem correct to say
that the Pelagian error embraced the notion of final admission to the
kingdom. Both the Pelagians and the Church agreed in excluding them
from the kingdom. As we saw, Augustine often used the Pelagians' ad-
missions on this point to embarrass them.

19. *PG* 46, c. 179, 183, 191.
20. *Ibid.*, c. 170.
21. *Ibid.*, c. 179.
22. *Ibid.*, c. 179.
23. E. V. McClear, "The Fall of Man and Original Sin in the Theology of
   Gregory of Nyssa," *Theological Studies*, IX (June, 1948); Johannes B.
   Aufhauser, *Die Heilslehre des hl. Gregor von Nyssa* (Munich, 1910).

24. *Oratio XL in Sanctum Baptisma, PG* 36, c. 359 ff.
25. *Ibid.,* c. 390.
26. *Topographia Christiana, PG* 88, c. 378.
27. *PG* 6, c. 1298; *PG* 28, 670-671.
28. *Quaestiones, PG* 89, c. 710.
29. *De Fide Liber Unus, PL* 65, c. 701.
30. *Poematum Libri VI, PL* 59, c. 370.
31. *Libri Moralium, PL* 75, c. 877.
32. *Sententiarum Libri Tres, PL* 83, c. 588.

CHAPTER II: SCHOLASTIC DEVELOPMENTS

1. A. Gaudel, "Péché Originel," *DTC* XII, c. 434.
2. *Ibid.,* c. 436.
3. *Liber de Conceptu Virginali,* XXIII, *PL* 158, c. 457.
4. J. Bellamy, "Baptême (Sort des enfants morts sans)," *DTC* II, c. 369.
5. *Sententiarum Libri Quatuor,* Lib. II, dist. 33, cap. 2.
6. Yves LeFèvre, *L'Elucidarium et Les Elucidaires* (Paris: de Boccard, 1954), p. 10.
7. *Ibid.,* p. 447.
8. *Ibid.,* p. 424, 450.
9. *Summa Theologica,* I, q. 1, a. 9, ad 1 um.
10. *Inferno:* canto 4.
11. *Scriptum super Lib. III Sententiarum,* d. 22, q. 2, art. 1, sol. 2.
12. Ambrosiaster.
13. *IV Sent.,* d. 54; *IV Sent.,* d. 1, a. 20.
14. *De Malo,* q. 5, art. 2.
15. *II Sent.,* d. 33, q. 2, art. 1.
16. *De Malo,* q. 5, a. 2.
17. *Ibid.*
18. *II Sent.,* d. 33, q. 2, a. 2.
19. *De Malo,* q. 5, a. 3.
20. *II Sent.,* d. 33, q. 2, a. 2.
21. Thomas Aquinas, Bonaventure, Alexander of Hales, Peter of Tartentaise, Richard Middleton, Giles of Rome, Guido de Orchellis, Peter Olivi.
22. *II Sent.,* d. 33, q. 3.
23. *II Sent.,* d. 33, a. 3, q. 2.
24. *IV Sent.,* d. 50, a. 5, q. 3.
25. *II Sent.,* d. 33, q. 1.
26. *Ibid.*
27. *II Sent.,* d. 33, a. 3, q. 2.
28. Thomas Aquinas, *II Sent.,* d. 33, q. 2, a. 2; Scotus, *II Sent.,* d. 33, q. 1; Durandus, *II Sent.,* d. 33, q. 3; Richard Middleton, *II Sent.,* d. 33, a. 3; q. 2; Peter of Tarentaise, *II Sent.,* d. 33, q. 2, a. 2.

29. Scotus, *II Sent.*, d. 33, q. 1; Bonaventure, *II Sent.*, d. 33, a. 3, q. 2.

30. "Majores Ecclesiae," *DB*, n. 410.

31. *Summa Theologiae*, II, tract. 17, q. 113.

32. *DB*, n. 464.

33. *Decretum pro Graecis, DB*, n. 693.

34. *DB*, n. 493a. Cf. F. Segarra, *Estudios Eclesiasticos*, 5:440.

CHAPTER III: THE AGE OF THE REFORM AND AFTER

1. *De Statu Futuro Puerorum sine Sacramento Decedentium* (Lyons, 1542).

2. L. Scarinci, *Giustizia primitiva e peccato originali secondo Ambrogio Catarino, O.P.; Studia Anselmiana,* 17.

3. Salmeron, *Comm. in Epist. ad Rom.* 5, disp. 48; Molina, *Concordia* (Paris, 1876), q. 23, a. 4, d. 1, memb. 9; Lessius, *De Perfectionibus Moribusque Divinis Opusculum,* lib. XIII, cap. 22.

4. *Commentaria ac Disputationes in Tertiam Partem D. Thomae,* quaest. 59, art. 6, disp. 57, sect. 6; quaest. 56, art. 2, disp. 50, sect. 3; quaest. 56, art. 2, disp. 50, sect. 5.

5. *De Peccato Originali,* disp. 9, sect. 6.

6. *Commentaria ac Disputationes in Tertiam Partem D. Thomae,* quaest. 59, art. 6, disp. 58, sect. 3.

7. *De Peccato Originali,* disp. 9, sect. 6, and *Commentaria ac Disputationes in Tertiam Partem,* quaest. 56, art. 2, disp. 50, sect. 5.

8. *Ibid.*

9. *Commentaria ac Disputationes in Tertiam Partem,* quaest. 56, art. 2, disp. 50, sect. 5.

10. A. Harnack, *History of Dogma,* trans. by W. M'Gilchrist (London: Williams and Norgate, 1889), Vol. VI, pp. 307 ff.

11. Among the professors at Louvain who were taken with the idea we find Conrius, Fabricius, Paludanus, Mercerus, Baius, Wiggers, Rampen, and Paludanus. F. Conrius, *Tractatus de Statu Parvulorum sine baptismo decedentium ex hac vita juxta sensum B. Augustini, compositus a F. Florentino Conrio, Hiberno, ad Archiepiscopatum Thuamensem ex Ordine Fr. Minor. Regular. Observ. assumpta* (Paris, 1641).

12. *Dogmata Theologica Dionysii Petavii e Societate Jesu,* rev. ed. J. B. Fournials (Paris: Vivès, 1865), Tome II, lib. IX, cap. IX-XI.

13. A. De Meyer, *Les Premières Controverses Jansénistes en France* (Louvain: J. Van Linthout, 1917).

14. *Augustinus,* Tome II, lib. ii, cap. 25, p. 181.

15. *Theses theologicae de gratia, libero arbitrio, praedestinatione, etc., in quibus doctrina theologorum societatis Jesu contra Conr. Jansenii Augustinum defenditur in VI capita divisae . . . Praeside R. P. Joanne de Jonghe, S.J. S.T. Prof., Defendet Joannes Groll ejusdem soc. Lovanii*

NOTES   *191*

in Collegio Soc. Jesu. Martii 1641 (Antverpiae, Apud Joannem Meursium, a. 1641), cap. ii, art. iv, p. 19.

16. *Histoire critique des principaux commentateurs du Nouveau Testament depuis le commencement du christianisme jusqu'à notre temps* (Rotterdam, 1693).

17. *Défense de la Tradition et des Saint Pères,* Part. II, liv. V, chap. II.

18. F. Cayré, "Augustinisme," *L'Année Théologique,* 2:79 (1941).

19. H. Noris, *Vindiciae Augustinianae Quibus S. Doctoris Scripta adversus Pelagianos, ac Semipelagianos a Recentiorum censuris asseruntur,* I, p. 14, 1.m.

20. *The History of the Popes from the Close of the Middle Ages* (St. Louis: Herder, 1938), Vol. XXIX, p. 363.

21. *Op. cit.,* p. 33.

22. *Ibid.*

23. *Jo. Laurentii Berti Florentini Fratris Eremitae Augustiniani Opus de Theologicis Disciplinis,* Romae, 1765, Sumptibus Josephi Remondini Veneti.

24. *Augustinianum Systema de Gratia ab iniqua bajani et janseniani erroris insumulatione vindicatum,* Romae, 1747, reprinted in *Opus de Theologicis Disciplinis,* Tome V, p. 63.

25. Manuel F. Miguelez, *Jansenismo y regalismo en España* (*datos para la historia*) (Valladolid, 1895), p. 308.

26. Letter of Benedict XIV to Cardinal Tencin of February 11, 1750; cf. Benedict XIV, *Correspondance de Benoit XIV,* ed. E. de Heeckeren, 2 vols. (Paris, 1912).

27. *Petri Tamburini Presbyteri S. Theol. Doctoris eiusdemq. Professoris in Seminario Brixiano De Summa Catholicae de Gratia Christi Doctrinae Praestantia Utilitate ac Necessitate,* Dissertatio (Brescia, 1771). We will use the seventh edition, Pavia, 1790.

28. G. Mantese, *Pietro Tamburini e Il Giansenismo Bresciano* (Brescia: Ancora, 1942), pp. 77-78.

29. *Op. cit.,* p. 54.

30. *Ibid.,* p. 113.

31. *Ibid.,* pp. 118-119.

32. P. Tamburini, *Analisi del libro delle Prescrizioni di Tertulliano* (Pavia, 1781), p. 172.

33. B. Matteucci, *Scipione Dè Ricci, Saggio Storico-Teologico sul Giansenismo Italiano* (Morcelliana, 1941), p. 178.

34. *Atti e decreti del concilio diocesano di Pistoia* (Florence, 1786), "Orazione al Sinodo," p. 110.

35. Cited by Miguelez, *op. cit.,* p. 73.

36. This letter of Paul III is reprinted in the *Opus de Theologicis Disciplinis,* Tome VII, p. 36.

37. This letter is also reprinted in the *Opus de Theologicis Disciplinis*, Tome I, pp. 167-168.

38. Benedict XIV, *Acta Benedicti XIV sive nondum sive sparsim edita nunc autem primum collecta cura Raphaelis de Martinis* (Naples, 1894), Vol. I, p. 554.

39. *Ibid.*

40. In a letter to Muratori Benedict explained that he had given a copy of his letter in confidence to the Procurator General. The latter thought that it would be a valuable preface to the works of Noris; the pope, however, told him that it was neither to be printed nor published. Two days later the procurator passed out copies of the letter without the pope's knowledge. Furious, Benedict forbade him ever to enter the Papal Palace again. *Cf.* Letter of Sept. 25, 1748, *Acta Benedicti XIV*, Vol. II, p. 396.

41. Letter of December 30, 1750 to de Saleons, *Acta Benedicti XIV*, Vol. II, p. 74.

42. *Acta,* letter of May 12, 1751, Vol. II, p. 412.

43. *Accademia dei Lincei: Biblioteca Corsiniana*, Rome, N. 1485, f. 193.

44. *Ibid.*

45. *Correspondance de Benoit XIV*, letter of June 25, 1749, Vol. I, p. 496.

46. Matteucci, *op. cit.*, p. 218, n. 2.

47. Cf. *MC*, v. 38, c. 1268.

CHAPTER IV: THE LAST THIRTY YEARS

1. *De Anima et ejus Origine*, I, 11, *PL* 44, c. 481.

2. Thomas Aquinas, *IV Sent.*, d. 6, q. 1, a. 2, ad 2; Alexander of Hales, *Summa*, IV, d. 6, q. 13, mem. 1, a. 1; Bonaventure, *IV Sent.*, d. 4, a. 5, q. 1, ad ult.

3. *Summa Aurea,* Lib. 3, tr. 3, cap. 4, q. 2.

4. *IV Sent.*, d. 6, q. 2, n. 12.

5. *IV Sent.*, d. 24, q. 1, a. 2, qla. 3.

6. A. Hernandez Santos, *Salvacion y paganismo* (Santander: Sal Terrae, 1960).

7. B. Webb, "Unbaptized Infants and the Quasi-Sacrament of Death," *The Downside Review* (Summer, 1953), pp. 243-257 (this is a refinement of H. Schell, *Katholische Dogmatik* [Paderborn, 1893], III, pp. 473-480); P. Glorieux, "Endurcissement final et grâces dernières," *Nouvelle Revue Théologique*, 59 (1932), pp. 865-892; "In hora mortis," *Mélanges des Sciences Religieuses,* 6 (1949), pp. 185-216; E. Sauras, "Los sacramentos de necessidad ante las circunstancias que impiden o anulan su administracion," *La Ciencia Tomista* (1957), pp. 37-73.

8. Cajetan; cf. his Commentary on the *Summa* of St. Thomas, III, q. 68, a. 2 and a. 11; Ch.-V. Heris, "Le salut des enfants morts sans baptême," *Maison Dieu* (1947), pp. 86-105; E. Boudes, "Réflexions sur la

solidarité des hommes avec le Christ," *Nouvelle Revue Théologique,* 71 (1949), pp. 589-604; G. Mulders, "Rond het Limbus vraagstuk," *Bijdragen,* 9 (1948), pp. 209-244.

9. M. Laurenge, "Esquisse d'une étude sur le sort des enfants morts sans baptême," *L'Année Théologique Augustinienne,* 12 (1952), pp. 145-185: Vincent Wilkin, *From Limbo to Heaven* (New York: Sheed and Ward, 1961).

10. Bibliographies of publications on this question have appeared in: Santos, *op. cit.,* pp. 705-710; *Nouvelle Revue Théologique,* 71 (1949), p. 589; *The Downside Review,* 72 (1954), pp. 359-390; *Gregorianum* (1954), pp. 406-456; *Bulletin Thomiste,* 9 (1954-56), pp. 854-871; *Revista Española de Teologia,* 21 (1961), pp. 3-4. A cross-section of the literature may be found in the following:

Diekhans, M., "Das Schicksal der ungetauften Kinder," *Theologie und Glaube* (1955), pp. 412-421.

Dyer, G., *The Denial of Limbo and the Jansenist Controversy* (Mundelein, Ill.: St. Mary of the Lake Seminary, 1955; Dissertationes ad Lauream. n. 24); "Limbo, a Theological Evaluation," *Theological Studies* (1958), pp. 32-49.

Fernandez, D., "Destino eterno de los niños que mueren sin bautismo," *Revista Española de Teologia* (1961), pp. 3-51.

Fernandez Jimenez, M., "A proposito de una teoria receinte sobre la suerte de los niños que mueren sin bautismo," *Revista Española de Teologia,* 15 (1955), pp. 271-292.

Garcia Plaza de San Luis, J., "Existe el Limbo de los niños?" *Revista Eclesiastica,* 10 (1936), pp. 113-155.

Gaudel, A., "Limbes," *DTC* IX, c. 760-772.

Greenstock, D., "En torno al problema de los niños que mueren sin bautismo," *Salmanticenses,* 2 (1955), pp. 245-264.

Gumpel, P., "Unbaptized Infants: May They Be Saved?" *The Downside Review,* 72 (1954), pp. 342-458.

Jellouschek, C. J., "Das Los der ohne Taufe sterbenden unmündigen Kinder," *Theologische-Praktische Quartalschrift,* 102 (1954), pp. 309-314.

Journet, C., *La Volonté divine salvifique sur les petits enfants* (Paris: Desclée, 1958).

Labourdette, M., "Problèmes d'eschatologie," *Revue Thomiste,* 54 (1954), pp. 658-675.

Landgraf, A., "Kindertaufe und Glaube in der Frühscholastik," *Gregorianum,* 9 (1928), pp. 337-372.

Leeming, B., "Is Their Baptism Really Necessary?" *The Clergy Review* (1954), pp. 66-85; 193-222; 321-340.

Lombardi, R., *The Salvation of the Unbeliever* (London: Burns Oates, 1956).

Lopez Martinez, N., *El mas alla de los niños* (Burgos, 1955).

Michel, A., *Enfants morts sans baptême* (Paris: Tequi, 1954).

Pacios, Lopez A., "La suerte de los niños muertos sin bautismo," *Revista Española de Teologia,* 14 (1954), pp. 41-57.

Renwart, L., "Le baptême des enfants et les limbes," *Nouvelle Revue Théologique* (1958), pp. 449-467.

Saiz, J. M., "En torno a los niños que mueren sin bautismo," *XIV Semana Española de Teologia* (Madrid, 1955), pp. 417-448.

Santos, A., "Infancia y bautismo," *Estudios Eclesiasticos* (1957), pp. 403-423.

Schuler, B., "Das Schicksal der ungetauften Kinder nach ihrem Tod," *Münchener Theologische Zeitschrift,* 7 (1956), pp. 120-128.

Stockums, W., *Das Los der ohne die Taufe sterbenden Kinder* (Freiburg im Breisgau: Herder, 1923).

Umberg, J., "Kajetans Lehre von der Kinderersatztaufe auf dem Trienter Konzil," *Zeitschrift für Katholische Theologie,* 39 (1915), pp. 452-464.

Van Roo, W., "Infants Dying without Baptism," *Gregorianum* (1954), pp. 406-473.

Zöttl, P., "Das Los der Kinder die ohne Taufe sterben," *Theologische-Praktische Quartalschrift* (1954), pp. 288-333.

Winklhofer, A., "Das Los der ungetauft verstorbenen Kinder," *Münchener Theologische Zeitschrift* (1956), pp. 45-60.

11. III, q. 70, a. 4, ad 2.
12. *De Sacramentis,* disp. III, sect. iii, n. 25.
13. Gousset, Martinet, Fischer, Fernandez, Hurter, Dublanchy are some of those listed by Santos as sympathetic to the Perrone opinion.
14. Cf. P. Horger, "Concilii Tridentini de necessitate baptismi doctrina in decreto de justificatione," *Antonianum,* 17, p. 290; Fernandez, *op. cit.,* p. 23.
15. *Hors d'église point de salut* (Paris: Tequi, 1927).
16. *Summa Theologiae,* III, q. 62, a. 6, ad 2.
17. Michel, *op. cit.,* p. 86.
18. Saiz, *op. cit.*
19. Karl Rahner's suggestions on a predisposition for justification may have some bearing here. Cf. *Theological Investigations* (Baltimore: Helicon, 1961), pp. 297-317.
20. Cf. an application of the Glorieux idea in J. B. Manya, "De ratione peccati poenam aeternam inducentis," in *Theologoumena* (Tortosa: Alguero et Baiges, 1946-   ), II, 1947.
21. Cf. R. Lombardi's detailed criticism, *op. cit.,* pp. 259-264.
22. *DB,* n. 693.
23. Fernandez Jimenez, *op. cit.,* p. 292.
24. *Op. cit.,* p. 66.
25. Wilkin, *op. cit.,* p. 40.
26. *Theological Studies,* June, 1962.

27. Wilkin, *op. cit.,* pp. 17-18.
28. *DB,* n. 795.
29. Gerson, *Sermo de Nativitate Virginis Mariae,* 2nd a consideratio; Biel, *IV Sent.,* d. 4, q. 2, dub. 2; Santos, *op. cit.;* Beni, *La vera chiesa* (Florence, 1953).

CHAPTER V: CONTEMPORARY DEBATE

1. *Concilii Tridentini Actorum pars alters* . . . edidit Stephanus Ehses (Freiburg im Breisgau: Herder, 1911), p. 239.
2. *Ibid.,* p. 792.
3. *Ibid.,* p. 856.
4. *Ibid.,* p. 854.
5. *Ibid.,* pp. 896-967.
6. *Ibid.,* pp. 961-962.
7. *Ibid.,* pp. 959-960.
8. *Ibid.,* p. 986.
9. *Ibid.,* pp. 986-990.
10. "Baptême d'après le Concile de Trent," *DTC* II, c. 306.
11. *Op. cit.,* pp. 94-95.
12. Horger, *op. cit.;* Santos, *op. cit.,* pp. 653 ff.
13. *DB,* n. 712.
14. *Op. cit.,* p. 164.
15. *Op. cit.,* p. 195.
16. *Op. cit.,* p. 164.
17. F. Floeri, *Augustinus Magister* (Paris, 1954), Vol. II, p. 761.
18. *PL* 54, c. 701.
19. *Ibid.,* 13, c. 1135.
20. *Ibid.,* 89, c. 503.
21. *Acta Apostolicae Sedis,* Dec. 20, 1951, p. 854. The pope's words are reminiscent of those of the Roman Catechism: "But infants since they are not capable of this desire are excluded, faith teaches us, from the kingdom of heaven . . . if they die unregenerated by baptism." *Catechismus Romanus,* pars ii, caput ii, n. xxiv.
22. F. X. Hürth, *Periodica,* 41 (1952), pp. 245-249.
23. Lopez Martinez, *op. cit.,* p. 87; J. Espeja, "La suerte de los niños que mueren sin bautismo," *La Ciencia Tomista* (1962), p. 594.
24. "Le salut des enfants morts sans baptême," *Revue Écclesiastique du Liége,* 38, p. 392.
25. Van Roo, *op. cit.,* p. 473; Fernandez, *op. cit.,* p. 37; Renwart, *op. cit.,* p. 466.
26. *Op. cit.,* p. 643.
27. *Op. cit.,* p. 84.
28. *Op. cit.,* p. 152.
29. *Op. cit.,* p. 466.
30. *Op. cit.,* pp. 534-535.
31. L. Richard, *Le Dogme de la rédemption* (Paris, 1932), p. 222; P.

Glorieux, *Introduction a l'étude du dogme* (Paris, 1948), p. 309; M. Schmaus, *Katholische Dogmatik* (Munich, 1952), IV, p. 161; Beni, *op. cit.*, pp. 427, 436, 444-445; A. Janssens, *Doopsel en Vormsel* (Kortrijk, 1938), pp. 14-16, 68-74; P. Pies, *Die Heilsfrage der Heiden* (Aachen, 1925); H. Schillebeeckx, *Die sacramentale Heilseconomie* (Antwerp, 1952); P. Minges, *Compendium theologiae dogmaticae specialis* (Regensburg, 1922), II; A. Bäuerle, "De Baptismo in voto quoad infantes praemorientes parentum piorum," *Estudis Franciscans*, 46, pp. 16-31; D. Feuling, *Einführung in das theologische Leben für weitere Kreise* (Salzburg, 1937); K. Rahner, *De gratia Christi: Summa praelectionum in usum privatum auditorum ordinata*; Oneoponte, ed. 3 a, 1950-51 (quoted by Gumpel, *op. cit.*, pp. 379-380); Sauras, *op. cit.*; Fernandez, *op. cit.*

32. *DB*, n. 410.
33. *Ibid.*, n. 464.
34. *Ibid.*, n. 493 a.
35. G. Hofman, "Formulae praeviae ad definitionem concilii Florentini de novissimis," *Gregorianum* (1937), p. 354, n. 29.
36. *DB*, n. 693.
37. *Op. cit.*, p. 209.
38. Fernandez, *op. cit.*, p. 35; Leeming, *op. cit.*, p. 210.
39. *Op. cit.*, p. 467.
40. *Op. cit.*, p. 435.
41. *DB*, n. 102.
42. *Op. cit.*, p. 471.
43. A. Michel, *L'Ami du Clergé*, 52, p. 660; Gaudel, "Limbes," *DTC* IX, c. 767.
44. J. Garcia Plaza de San Luis, *op. cit.*, p. 113.
45. Sauras, *op. cit.*, p. 52.
46. Fernandez, *op. cit.*, p. 7.
47. *In primam partem S. Thomae*, disp. 96, c. 2 and 3.
48. *Op. cit.*
49. *Ibid.*
50. D. Fernandez, *op. cit.*, p. 8.
51. Michel, *Enfants morts sans baptême*, p. 69.
52. *PL* 43, c. 172-177.
53. *Ibid.*, 16, c. 1374.
54. *DB*, n. 388.
55. *Ibid.*, n. 413.
56. *Summa*, III, q. 68, a. 2.
57. *DB*, n. 796.
58. *Collectio Lacensis*, V, 320.
59. *Op. cit.*, p. 466.